THE POEMS

OF

Aemilia Lanyer

WOMEN WRITERS IN ENGLISH
1350–1850

GENERAL EDITOR
Susanne Woods

MANAGING EDITOR
Elaine Brennan

EDITORS
Patricia Caldwell
Stuart Curran
Margaret J. M. Ezell
Elizabeth H. Hageman
Elizabeth D. Kirk

WOMEN WRITERS PROJECT
Brown University

THE POEMS

OF

Aemilia Lanyer

*   *   *

Salve Deus Rex Judæorum

EDITED BY

Susanne Woods

New York   Oxford

OXFORD UNIVERSITY PRESS

1993

Oxford University Press

Oxford   New York   Toronto
Delhi   Bombay   Calcutta   Madras   Karachi
Kuala Lumpur   Singapore   Hong Kong   Tokyo
Nairobi   Dar es Salaam   Cape Town
Melbourne   Auckland   Madrid
and associated companies in
Berlin   Ibadan

Published by Oxford University Press, Inc.,
198 Madison Avenue, New York, New York 10016-4314

Oxford is a registered trademark of Oxford University Press

Library of Congress Cataloging-in-Publication Data

Lanyer, Aemilia.
[Works 1993]
The poems of Aemilia Lanyer: Salve Deus Rex Judaeorum /
Aemilia Lanyer: edited by Susanne Woods.
p.   cm.   -- (Women writers in English 1350–1850)
1. Christian poetry, English. Women—England—Poetry.
I. Woods, Susanne. 1943–   . II. Title.   III. Series.
PR2296.L27S2 1993 821'.3--dc20   92-16761
ISBN 0-19-508037-8 (cloth)
ISBN 0-19-508361-X (paper)

This volume was supported in part by the National Endowment
for the Humanities, an independent federal agency.

Printing (last digit):
20 19 18 17 16 15 14 13 12

Printed in the United States of America
on acid-free paper

For Anne Shaver

CONTENTS

Salve Deus Rex Judæorum

FOREWORD

Women Writers in English 1350–1850 presents texts of cultural and literary interest in the English-speaking tradition, often for the first time since their original publication. Most of the writers represented in the series were well known and highly regarded until the professionalization of English studies in the later nineteenth century coincided with their excision from canonical status and from the majority of literary histories.

The purpose of this series is to make available a wide range of unfamiliar texts by women, thus challenging the common assumption that women wrote little of real value before the Victorian period. While no one can doubt the relative difficulty women experienced in writing for an audience before that time, or indeed have encountered since, this series shows that women nonetheless had been writing from early on and in a variety of genres, that they maintained a clear eye to readers, and that they experimented with an interesting array of literary strategies for claiming their authorial voices. Despite the tendency to treat the powerful fictions of Virginia Woolf's *A Room of One's Own* (1928) as if they were fact, we now know, against her suggestion to the contrary, that there were many "Judith Shakespeares," and that not all of them died lamentable deaths before fulfilling their literary ambitions.

This series is unique in at least two ways. It offers, for the first time, concrete evidence of a rich and lively heritage of women writing in English before the mid-nineteenth century, and it is based on one of the most sophisticated and forward-looking electronic resources in the world: the Brown University Women Writers Project textbase (full text database) of works by early women writers. The Brown University Women Writers Project (WWP) was established in 1988 with a grant from the National Endowment for the Humanities, which continues to assist in its development.

Women Writers in English 1350–1850 is a print publication project derived from the WWP. It offers lightly-annotated versions based on single good copies or, in some cases, collated versions of texts with more complex editorial histories, normally in their original spelling. The editions are aimed at a wide audience, from the informed undergraduate through professional students of literature, and they attempt to include the general reader who is interested in exploring a fuller tradition of early texts in English than has been available through the almost exclusively male canonical tradition.

SUSANNE WOODS
General Editor

ACKNOWLEDGMENTS

Producing a book is always a cooperative project; producing a series of books such as Women Writers in English becomes more of a cooperative crusade. What began as a small specialized research project has developed into an adventure in literature, computing, and publishing far beyond our initial abstract conception.

At Brown University, many administrators have given the Women Writers Project invaluable support, including President Vartan Gregorian, Provost Frank Rothman, Dean of the Faculty Bryan Shepp, and Vice President Brian Hawkins. Vital assistance has come from the English Department, including chairs Walter Davis, Stephen M. Foley, and Elizabeth D. Kirk, and from staff members at Computing and Information Services, particularly Don Wolfe, Allen Renear, and Geoffrey Bilder. Maria Fish has staffed the Women Writers Project office through crises large and small.

At Oxford University Press, Elizabeth Maguire, Claude Conyers, and Ellen Barrie have been patient, helpful, and visionary, all at the same time.

Ashley Cross, Julia Deisler, and Lisa Gim shared with me their excitement about teaching early women writers, as have many other faculty members and graduate students at Brown and elsewhere. My friends and colleagues locally in Brown's Computing in the Humanities Users Group and internationally in the Text Encoding Initiative, especially Michael Sperberg-McQueen, have stimulated my thinking about texts and the electronic uses and encoding of texts. Syd Bauman and Grant Hogarth have sustained me in the computer and publishing aspects of the project.

Students are the life's blood of the Women Writers Project, and all of the students who have passed through our offices are part of this volume. Most particularly, among those who worked on *Salve Deus* were Elizabeth Adams, Sarah Finch Brown, Elizabeth Carroll, Ashley Cross, Julia Flanders, Sharon Garrick, Lisa Gim, Thomas Harshman,

Daniel J. Horn, Jason R. Loewith, Carole E. Mah, Eowyn A. Rieke, and Elizabeth Soucar.

Other students have contributed mightily to the spirit and vitality of the WWP: Jennifer Bomze, Carolyn Cannuscio, Lisa Chick, Amanda Deaver, John Fitzgerald, Amy Frisch, Nina Greenberg, Deborah Hirsch, Jennifer Hofer, Mithra Irani, Anthony Lioi, Leslie Stern, Susan B. Taylor, Michele Tepper, Elizabeth Weinstock, and Andrea Weissman.

My personal thanks go especially to Sarah Finch Brown and Julia Flanders for their meticulous scholarship, extraordinary dedication to the project, and their patience through the final stages of production details.

ELAINE BRENNAN
Managing Editor

ACKNOWLEDGMENTS

I am grateful for the help and encouragement of a large number of people who feel, as I do, that Aemilia Lanyer's work substantially changes our perspective on the English Renaissance. My thanks to Suzanne W. Hull, who started us all in this direction; Barbara Lewalski, who showed and still shows the way; Gary Waller, who was one of the first to take these women seriously; Josephine Roberts and Margaret Hannay, whose works on Lady Mary Wroth and the Countess of Pembroke provide continuing inspiration; Elaine Hobby for her scholarly enthusiasm and integrity; and the members of the Harvard and New York seminars on women in the Renaissance, who contributed so much to my thinking about Lanyer. I have also received substantial inspiration and information from my students at Brown University and Franklin and Marshall College and from discussions with countless colleagues.

The research team of the Brown-NEH Women Writers Project has been responsible, as a group and individually, for recovering early women writers in English and for overseeing the development of this series. We made all the major decisions together, and whatever is good about this edition and the series owes much to them. I am grateful to Patricia Caldwell, Margaret Ezell, and Elizabeth Kirk, and most especially to Elizabeth Hageman, who oversaw every part of this book, and to Stuart Curran, one of my best friends for more years than either of us cares to contemplate. The Project's key player, Elaine Brennan, has literally made this book possible. I also want to thank James P. Miller, my editorial assistant and Hackman Research Fellow at Franklin and Marshall College, who contributed a great deal to the notes in this edition. Peter Blayney very kindly reviewed the textual introduction. Elizabeth Maguire of Oxford University Press has been friend and cheering section as well as visionary in helping us all turn the Women Writers Project into printed volumes. Any errors in this work are my own.

Grants from the National Endowment for the Humanities have been a crucial piece of all of the work of the Women Writers Project, including this edition. Brown University Provosts Maurice Glicksman and Frank Rothman assured institutional support for the Project during its five initial years; without their help, this book and many others would not have been possible. I am also grateful to President Vartan Gregorian of Brown for his visionary leadership and for offering me a sabbatical in Oxford in the fall of 1990, and to Susan Hockey and Marilyn Deegan of the Humanities Centre at the Oxford University Computing Service for making me a welcomed colleague during that time and since. President Richard Kneedler of Franklin and Marshall College has generously provided me with time and resources (not always convenient to the College) to complete this work.

For access to manuscripts and editions, I am grateful to the British Library, the Bodleian Library, the Avon County Library in Bath, the library of the Victoria and Albert Museum, the Chapin Library of Williams College, the Guildhall Library, the Public Record Office, and the Greater London History Library; for particular help with sometimes odd questions, I especially thank the superb staffs of the Henry E. Huntington Library and the Folger Shakespeare Library. Between them, these two great institutions have four of the nine extant copies of the *Salve Deus Rex Judæorum*. The maps in this edition are reproduced by the kind permission of The Guildhall Library, City of London, and the Museum of London, and are taken from the *Collection of Early Maps of London, 1553–1667*, introduction by John Fisher and published by the Guildhall Library.

Anne Shaver, to whom this book is dedicated, has been friend, scholar, and partner in the development of this edition and in many other things. She continues to be a fountain of ideas and support.

SUSANNE WOODS

INTRODUCTION

Aemilia Lanyer's life, like the lives of the vast majority of her contemporaries, is mostly shrouded in the indifference of the past. Various public records offer some information, and we know or can reasonably induce more from two additional sources. The astrologer Simon Forman (1552–1611) kept a professional diary and detailed casebooks about the people who came to him for consultation, with Lanyer among those who visited him several times in 1597. Read carefully and critically, these works provide a close glimpse of one period of her life. In addition, Lanyer's poems assert or suggest some autobiographical facts, although these should be seen within the conventions of the volume in which they are printed. Together these materials sketch a portrait of an intelligent, attractive, strong-minded woman whose life on the fringes of Elizabethan and Jacobean court society gave her some opportunity for education and advancement, but whose ambitions outstripped her social class and financial resources. She developed a distinct poetic voice, and may have been the first Englishwoman to publish a full edition of poems and to claim for herself a professional poetic voice, as her male contemporaries (such as Ben Jonson) were just beginning to do.

She was born Aemilia Bassano, the daughter of court musician Baptist Bassano, described in his will as a "native of Venice," and of Margaret Johnson, his common law wife.[1] Aemilia was christened in the

---

1. Her father's will, witnessed 3 January 1576, and proved 7 July that same year, professes him to have been "a native of venice and one of the the Musitions of our Sovereigne Ladye the Quenes majestie." He first provides for his burial, and next leaves "to Emelia Bassany Daughter of the bodie of Margarett Bassany also Margarett Johnson my reputed wieff the some of one hundreth poundes of lawefull money of England to be paide at her full age of one and twentie yeres or daye of mariage whether shall first happen." He names his wife executrix of the will, directs her in providing the hundred pounds to their daughter, and gives to Margaret the use of the money if his daughter should die before becoming eligible for it (London Public Record Office [hereafter PRO], Prob. 11/58, f. 153). Her mother may have been the Margaret Johnson baptised in 1544 at St. Margaret's, Westminster (International Genealogical Index, published by the Church of Jesus Christ of the Latter Day Saints, located at the Greater London History Library; hereafter referred to as IGI, Greater London). All dates in this introduction are new style.

parish church of St. Botolph, Bishopsgate, 27 January 1569,[2] just outside the London wall near the developing suburb of The Spital, where her father had long-term leases on three houses.[3] A detailed map of the area from around 1559 (see Map A, xliii) shows the church next door to a group of houses with a substantial garden, the "Giardin di Piero," and, next after that, the buildings and gardens of St. Mary of Bethlehem, the notorious "Bedlam."[4] Lanyer's older contemporary, John Stow (1525?–1605), describes the area as it was not long after her birth:

> The parish church of St. Buttolph without Bishopsgate [is] in a fair churchyard, adjoining to the town ditch, upon the very bank thereof, but of old time inclosed with a comely wall of brick, lately repaired by Sir William Allen, Mayor, in the year 1571, because he was born in that parish, where also he was buried. ... Next unto the parish church of St. Buttolph is a fair inn for receipt of travelers; than an hospital of St. Mary of Bethlehem, founded by Simon Fitz Mary, one of the sheriffs of London, in the year 1246: he founded it to have been a priory of canons ... and King Edward III, granted a protection ... the 14th year of his reign. It was an hospital for distracted people.[5]

Across from the church, according to Stow, was another "large inn for receipt of travellers, ... called the Dolphin, of such a sign," and up the road is "the late dissolved priory and hospital, commonly called St Mary Spittle." This large and prosperous property had been taken over by Henry VIII when he dissolved the monasteries (1535–40), and it is possible that Baptist Bassano may have received his leases directly or indirectly from the dissolution. Stow says that in Elizabethan times "in place

---

2. The baptismal record is of "Emillia Baptist," but this is very probably the right person (Parish Register of St. Botolph's Bishopsgate, Guildhall Library 4515/1).

3. Bassano left to his wife and residually to his two daughters "the rentes yssued and proffitte of my three messuages or Tenements with their appurtenances situate and rentes yssued and being in the Parrisshe of St. Bottolphes withoute Bisshopsgate London nere unto the Spittle ... and also use and occupation of the said three Tenements" (PRO 11/58 f. 154).

4. All maps are from *A Collection of Early Maps of London 1553–1667*, intro. John Fisher (Lyme, Kent: Harry Margary, in association with the Guildhall Library, London, 1981), used by permission.

5. John Stow, *A Survay of London Conteyning the Originall, Antiquity, Increase, Moderne estate, and description of that City, written in the yeare 1598 ... Since by the same Author increased* (London, 1603); Everyman ed. (London: J. M. Dent, 1956), 148–49.

of this hospital, and near adjoining, are now many fair houses built for receipt and lodging of worshipful persons." Or it may be that Bassano's houses were among those newly built by the nearby field known as "The Spital."[6] The area of Aemilia's birth was therefore an old suburb adjacent to London, newly developing under Elizabethan prosperity.

What may have begun as a life of some privilege had setbacks even before Aemilia's father died on 11 April 1576, when she was seven. According to Forman's records of Lanyer's visit to him on 17 May 1597, she told him that "her father died when she was yonge and he had mis fortune /. and her mother did outlive her father—and the welth of her father failed before he died & he began to be miserable in his estate."[7]

Bassano's will nonetheless left his daughter a dowry of "one hundreth poundes of lawefull money of England to be paide at her full age of one and twentie yeres or daye of mariage" and the rents and use of the three houses, to be divided with an older sister, Angela Holland, at the death of her mother.[8] About her sister Angela, by 1576 married to "Joseph Hollande gentleman," we hear nothing more.[9]

After her father's death Aemilia continued to have access to court circles. The poem dedicated to "the Ladie Susan, Countesse Dowager of Kent" describes Lady Susan as "the Mistris of my youth. / The noble guide of my ungovern'd dayes," and Lanyer reports to Simon Forman that "she [Lanyer] was brought up on the bankes of Kente."[10] Access to this noble household was very likely access as well to the education that informs Lanyer's poems, including some familiarity with the classical tradition and with the techniques of rhetoric.

---

6. Stow, 150–51; see Map A.

7. Bodleian Manuscript Ashmole (Hereafter BOD MS Ashmole) 226, f. 95[v]. This manuscript contains Forman's casebooks, which have almost daily entries. He also kept a professional textbook/diary, titled *Geomantica*, with more extensive and less frequent entries (BOD MS Ashmole 354).

8. PRO Prob. 11/58 f. 153–4.

9. Her husband may be the "Joseph Holland, gentleman" mentioned by Stow, 22.

10. "To the Ladie Susan," lines 1–2; BOD MS Ashmole 226, f. 110[v].

In 1587 Aemilia's mother died,[11] by which time or shortly thereafter her eighteen-year-old daughter had come to the attention of another important Tudor aristocrat. Henry Cary, Lord Hunsdon, was then Queen Elizabeth's Lord Chamberlain. Though forty-five years older than Aemilia, he was a prominent courtier and a patron of the arts (including Shakespeare's theater company, the Lord Chamberlain's Men). On three different occasions during her 1597 visits to Forman, Lanyer recalled her life with Hunsdon and lamented her necessary marriage to Alphonso Lanyer, thus suggesting that she continued to long for the glamorous world the Lord Chamberlain had provided:

> (May 17): She was pa[ra]mour to my old L. of huns-Dean that was L Chamberline and was maintained in great pride and yt seames that being with child she was for collour maried to a minstrell.

> (June 3): [she] hath bin married 4 years / The old Lord Chamberlain kept her longue She was maintained in great pomp. ... she hath 40£ a yere & was welthy to him that maried her in monie & Jewells.

> (September 2): She hath been favored much of her mati [majestie, Queen Elizabeth] and of mani noble men & hath had gret giftes & bin moch made of . and a nobleman that is ded hath Loved her well & kept her and did maintain her longe but her husband hath delte hardly with her and spent and consumed her goods and she is nowe ... in debt.[12]

Aemilia's marriage had taken place when she was 23, on 18 October 1592, in another St. Botolph's church, the nearby St. Botolph's, Aldgate, in whose parish several of her father's relatives resided. The contemporary record reads, "Alfonso Lanyer one of the Queenes musitions & Emilia bassano Maryed the 18 Daye of october."[13] In early 1593 she had a son, whom she named Henry, presumably after his actual father, the Lord Chamberlain.

---

11. Both Baptist Bassano and Margaret Johnson were buried at St. Botolph's, Bishopsgate—he on 11 April 1576, and she on 7 July 1587 (Guildhall Library 4515/1).

12. BOD MS Ashmole 226 ff. 95^v, 110^v, 201.

13. Register General of St. Botolph's Aldgate, 1571–1593, Guildhall Library 9221.

Aemilia Lanyer's consultations with Simon Forman began on 13 May 1597. In a short entry he notes an apparently brief visit from "Millia Lanier of 29 [sic] yeares in Longditch at Westmenster," which reveals that by then she was residing in the City of Westminster, on the far side of the City of London from the parish of her birth.[14] There was in that time a "long ditch" in the northwest area of the smaller city, "so called," according to Stow, "for that the same almost insulateth the City of Westminster."[15] The area in which Lanyer lived was near St. James Park, then a royal deer park, and not far from the royal court (see Map B, xliv).

Lanyer's subsequent visits to Forman offer an interesting glimpse of her life and concerns over several months in 1597, though filtered by Forman's own accounts of increasing interest in her as a possible sexual partner. The closest we come to daily events in her life, Forman's accounts of these visits are worth analyzing in some detail. His notes give us a picture not only of the background information that Lanyer reported, but of the flow of her visits and their effect on one popular figure of the time; Forman's casebooks show him to have been a successful astrologer and consultant on a wide variety of matters to a large number of people from across social classes.

---

14. BOD MS Ashmole 226 f. 93[V]. A. L. Rowse originally misread this entry as a visit from one "William Lanier," and used that to begin his case that Aemilia was Shakespeare's "Dark Lady" (A. L. Rowse, *Shakespeare's Sonnets: The Problems Solved*, London, 1973, xxxiv–xliii). He apparently realized his mistake early on, since the next year he pursues his case, but without claiming that she was married to a "William" (Rowse, *Simon Forman: Sex and Society in Shakespeare's Age*, London, 1974, 96–117). Rowse cites many of the same diary entries I cite in this introduction, but he omits some important references, assumes that Aemilia probably slept with Forman (though Forman never claims so), and makes some errors in transcription. Rowse deserves thanks for directing us to evidence about Lanyer's life, though his work is riddled with errors and was written in distracting service to the thesis that she was the "Dark Lady" of Shakespeare's sonnets. From the slimmest evidence—the association with the Lord Chamberlain, Simon Forman's recorded attendance at Shakespearean plays, Lanyer's Italian background and therefore presumably dark complexion—Rowse weaves a romance of the *Salve Deus Rex Judæorum* as Lanyer's revenge for the 1609 publication of Shakespeare's sonnets. Lanyer may have known Shakespeare, since the world of middle class artistic servants of the crown was not large, but there is no direct evidence, and Rowse's fantasy has tended to obscure Lanyer as a poet.

15. Stow, 403.

Lanyer returned to Forman on 17 May 1597, four days after her first visit, this time for the full casting of her horoscope. Forman's practice was to record from two to four different client visits on a folio page of his casebook, with four small horoscopes often quartering the page, but on this second visit Lanyer merits a full page, on which Forman casts both her current horoscope and one "for her life past." She is noted as "Emilia Bassana," and off to the right he adds "also is Lanier." She is described as "of 27 yeares [she was 28] 2 [second] filia [daughter] Baptista Bassano et Margarete Johnson." It is here that Forman records Lanyer's "hard fortune in her youth" and her marriage of convenience to Alphonso.

On 3 June 1597, Lanyer again visited Forman, who this time records specific concerns. She has come, "the wife for the husband," to inquire "when her husband shall have the suit." A more personal issue also emerges. "She seams to be with child of 12 daies or 12 weakes moch pain in the left syd." She is prone to miscarriages. Forman twice records in this entry that "she hath mani fals conceptions," or unsuccessful pregnancies. On this occasion Aemilia elaborates on her past with the Lord Chamberlain and the relative wealth she brought to Alphonso. Forman also reports that "she hath som thing in her mind she would have don for hir" and that "she can hardly kepe secret / she was very brave in youth. ... She hath a sonne his name is henri."[16] Two weeks later, on 16 June, she arrived at Forman's house again: "Mrs. Lanier for her husband. wh[eth]er he shall com to Any preferment before he com hom Again or no. & how he shall speed ... & wh[eth]er he shall com home Again or no."[17] A later entry in another Forman volume clarifies this earlier one by explaining that Aemilia's "husband was gone to Sea with therle [the Earl] of Essex in hope to be knighted."[18] Though Alphonso's chances for success remain a continuing concern in her encounters with Forman, on 16 June Aemilia also reports "moch pain in the bottom of the body womb stomacke & hed & [wills?] to vomit." For her suffering

---

16. BOD MS Ashmole 226, f. 95^v, 110^v.   17. BOD MS Ashmole 226, f. 122^v.
18. BOD MS Ashmole 354, f. 246; entry dated 2 Sept. 1597.

Forman (or possibly someone else) "gave her appothic drink to her pur-
gation."[19]

By her next visit, on 2 September 1597, Aemilia apparently felt better,
and Forman seems to have believed that she might be interested in him.
It is evident from this entry, and from three September entries in a different volume (Forman's *Geomantica*, see below), that Forman, who considered himself a ladies' man, finds her attractive. She has come to ask the
astrologer "whether she shall be a Ladi. & how she shall speed." He again
records her report of good favor from Queen Elizabeth and happy life
with the Lord Chamberlain, adding here that "her husband hath delte
hardly with her and spent and consumed her goods and she is nowe very
needy and in debte & it seams for Lucrese[20] sake wilbe a good fellowe for
necessity doth compell." In a different slant of writing that suggests a
later entry, he adds the only recorded statement about her appearance:
"She hath a wart or moulle in the pit of the throte or ner yt."[21]

On this same day Forman casts a horoscope based on Aemilia's questions, and concludes, "She shalbe A Ladie or attain to som further dignitie /. He shall speed well & be knighted hardly [i.e., with difficulty]
but shall get lyttle substaunce And the tyme shall com she shall rise too
degrees but hardly by this man. but yt seems he will not lyve too yeres
after he com home. And yet ther shall som good fortune fall on her in
shorte tyme." Though we have insufficient records to tell whether any
of his predictions came to pass, we do know he was wrong on the big
issues. Alphonso Lanyer was never knighted. Aemilia never rose
socially. And Alphonso survived Forman's two-year death sentence, living until 1613.

The second volume that contains September 1597 entries related to
Aemilia Lanyer is Forman's *Geomantica*, a manuscript textbook and
analysis of astrological figures in which he also presents a diary of set

---

19. BOD MS Ashmole 226, f. 122^{v}.

20. **Lucrese:** lucre, money. Possibly also a cryptic reference to Lucrece, whose rape by a
member of the ruling family caused the downfall of early imperial Rome.

21. BOD MS Ashmole 226, f. 201.

pieces of problems and questions his horoscopes are supposed to help answer. An entry for 2 September appears under the page heading "Of digniti and office," and poses the following case: "A Gentlewoman whose husband was gone to Sea with therle of Essex in hope to be knighted thought ther was Lyttle cause whie he should. Demaund in his absence wh[eth]er she shall be a Ladie or noe ... 1597 the 2 Septemb."[22] Two charts are cast side by side below this question, the first evidently Alphonso's. Over the second is written "Emilia Lanier." Under the first Forman concludes, "he was not knighted nor yet worthy thereof." Under Aemilia's he has added, "she shall not nor was not nor worthi therof."

Two other entries in the *Geomantica* portray Forman's efforts to initiate sexual relations. Throughout the diaries, "halek" is the euphemism he uses to indicate the sex act. On 11 September he heads a page with the query, "Beste to doe A thinge or noe," and poses the following situation: "A certain man longed to see A gentlewoman whom he loved & desired to halek with. and because he could not tell howe to com to her & whether he should be welcom to her or noe, Moved this question wh[eth]er yt were best to send to her to knowe howe she did. and therbi to tri wh[eth]er she wold byd the messaunger byd his mrs round to him or noe. Thinking therby what he myght goodlye bolden therby to see her."[23]

Two charts appear side by side under this entry, the first headed "Lanier," and the second headed with a date nine days later than the 11 September question, "1597 20 Sept." followed by the Mars symbol—presumably Forman's own chart. Beneath Lanyer's he has written, "The partie sent his servaunte by who she sente word that if his mr came he should be welcom. & he wente and supped wth her and staid all night. and she was familiar & friendlie to him in all things. But only she

22. BOD MS Ashmole 354, f. 246. See notes 7 and 18, above. I am grateful to Susan Cerasano for generously sharing her transcriptions of several of these Ashmole 354 passages, which in most cases agree with mine. In the few places where we disagree, I have sometimes been persuaded by her reading and sometimes stayed with my own.

23. BOD MS Ashmole 354, f. 250.

wold not halek. Yet he tolde all parts of her body wilingly. & kyssed her often but she wold not doe in any wise. Wherupon … he departed friendes." Under his own chart, he concludes, "yt is not best to do it. … she would not … it not / he had great trouble about yt and it confused him." Forman adds to this in a hand that might be later still, "but not [interdicting?] to com at her Again in haste, but yet they were frendes again afterward but he never obteyned his purpose & she was a hore and delt evill with him after."

Forman's frustration is evident as he reports that Lanyer was friendly to him, apparently enjoyed his company, let him kiss her, but would not "halek" and "he never obteyned his purpose." His reaction suggests that he is not interested in friendship on her terms. His calling her a "hore" who "delt evill with him" must be taken in the context of his disappointment. If these visits to Lanyer's home are real, and not part of what may well be Forman's rich fantasy life, then they were troubling encounters that may have continued for at least a short time.

Under another page headed, "Best to doe a thinge or noe," Forman poses a "Question 1597 the 23 Septem … Best to goe to Laniere todae or noe." Under his own chart he concludes, "I went not for as I was about to go my [ost?] came & we went presently to elton /. She next daie at after non she sent her maid to me & I went with her to her." It is difficult to say whether or not this last refers to Lanyer. The horoscope next to Forman's is of another gentlewoman, "Jone Harrington," with whom he visited "& did Halek" on 29 October 1597.

Forman's last certain reference to Lanyer in 1597 is an undated note following others dated 29 September in his casebook. It says only, "Emilia Lanie the daughter of Baptista & Margaret Bassana."[24] She may have stopped by, but Forman was apparently in no mood to cast her horoscope. Rowse imagines that she came for purposes of sex; one might better imagine that she came for a consultation, but that the sexually rejected Forman did not want to spend time with her.

---

24. BOD MS Ashmole 226, f. 222$^\text{v}$.

Rowse has made much of these September entries, seeing in them evidence of Lanyer's loose character and Forman's irresistibility to women. There is, however, nothing in them to suggest Forman ever did manage to "halek" with Lanyer. His casebooks and especially the *Geomantica* are peppered with accounts of his sexual encounters, about which he is quite explicit except for the curious "halek" euphemism; nevertheless he records about Lanyer only his own hope and disappointment. That disappointment, rather than the success followed by disgust that Rowse unaccountably assumes, may better explain Forman's last reference to Aemilia Lanyer. Just over two years later, on 7 January 1600, Forman casts his own horoscope to try to discover "at 5 pm 7 Jan to know whi Mrs. Laniere sent for me et quid a sequiter / wh[eth]er she Entends Any mor Villani or noe."[25]

Aemilia Lanyer fades from view in Forman's life, but not without leaving a strong impression. We learn from Forman that she was ambitious, attractive, and strong minded. She had a wart or mole near the pit of her neck. She was subject to miscarriages, and may have gone to Forman as much for help with this problem as for a prediction of Alphonso's success.

Two slightly later pieces of documentary information record the baptism and burial of Lanyer's daughter, Odillya. She is listed as the daughter of "Alphonso Laniere" in a baptism recorded in December 1598, at St. Margaret's, Westminster—the parish church we would expect for residents of Westminster.[26] Forman's record that Aemilia Lanyer had "mani fals conceptions" makes this an important event; in a pregnancy whose inception corresponds with her husband's return from the Essex expedition, she apparently at last was able to carry a child to term. Her book of poems suggests strongly that Lanyer's female identity was important to her, and as far as we know Odillya was her first and only daughter. It seems likely that this birth of a female child after a history of miscarriages had a strong impact on

---

25. BOD MS Ashmole 236, f. 5.   26. IGI, Greater London.

Lanyer's sense of her own continuing identity, and it may even be that her daughter's name derives from combining "ode" with her own name, "Aemilia," perhaps reflecting her developing identity as a poet. Whatever the reasons, her child's death nine months later was a profound enough experience for Lanyer to have her buried not from the local parish church of St. Margaret's where Odillya had been baptised, but from St. Botolph's Bishopsgate, the church all the way back across the city of London, and back in time from Aemilia's current world. The family church and parish area fade finally from her life after "Odillya Lanyer bur the 6 of Sep," 1599.[27]

Between 1600 and the entry of Lanyer's poems into the Stationers' Register on 2 October 1610, Alphonso Lanyer received in 1604 from King James a patent that granted him the income from the weighing of hay and grain, and Aemilia spent some time before 1609 at the royal country house estate, Cookham, with Margaret, Countess of Cumberland, and her daughter, Anne Clifford.[28] The patent provided some steady income, while the time spent at Cookham, and Lanyer's conversations with Margaret Clifford, must count as among the most powerful experiences of Lanyer's life, if only through their impetus in creating much of the poetry in the *Salve Deus*.

"The Description of Cooke-ham" was apparently written sometime between 25 February 1609 when Anne Clifford became Countess of Dorset (her marriage is acknowledged in the poem) and the poem's publication in late 1610. In the first several lines of "Cooke-ham" Lanyer seems to credit her sojourn at that great estate with inspiring her poem on the Passion:

---

27. Guildhall Library 4515/1.

28. S P 14 (James I), 9/20; Barbara Lewalski notes that Cookham was a crown manor leased to Margaret's brother, William Russell of Thornhaugh, "and occupied by the Countess of Cumberland at some periods during her estrangement from her husband in the years before his death in 1605, and perhaps just after. Anne Clifford's diary records a visit to Cookham in 1603" (Lewalski, "Imagining Female Community: Aemilia Lanyer's Poems," *Writing Women in Jacobean England,* Cambridge: Harvard Univ. Press, 1993, 212–41, n. 11). She also points out that Anne Clifford's marriage establishes the *terminus ad quem* for Lanyer's Cookham visit.

> Farewell (sweet *Cooke-ham*) where I first obtain'd
> Grace from that Grace where perfit Grace remain'd;
> And where the Muses gave their full consent,
> I should have powre the virtuous to content:
> Where princely Palace will'd me to indite,
> The sacred Storie of the Soules delight.   (lines 1–6)

Lanyer also claims, as she does in the "Salve Deus" poem and in her dedications to the Countess Dowager of Cumberland, that Margaret's direct influence was the efficient cause of Lanyer's godly verse. Whether the references in "Cooke-ham" to the Countess's inspiration are meant to refer to only that poem or additionally to the "Salve Deus," "Cooke-ham" appears to chronicle, if also to idealize, a time of rich poetic activity.

Yet that time has passed. In the valedictory mood that pervades "The Description of Cooke-ham," Lanyer urges the Countess to think of the place as a dim and transient earthly image of paradise, and again alludes to Margaret's role as poetic influence:

> Yet you (great Lady) Mistris of that Place,
> From whose desires did spring this worke of Grace;
> Vouchsafe to thinke upon those pleasures past,
> As fleeting worldly Joyes that could not last:
> Or, as dimme shadowes of celestiall pleasures.   (lines 11–15)

Whenever and for however long Lanyer was at Cookham, she claims in the poem a close and affectionate relationship that has since been disrupted. The social distance between them was very great, as Lanyer acknowledges:

> Unconstant Fortune, thou art most too blame,
> Who casts us downe into so lowe a frame:
> Where our great friends we cannot dayly see,
> So great a diffrence is there in degree.   (lines 103–6)

Although Aemilia's early years around the court, her upbringing in the household of the Countess of Kent, and her time with Lord

Hunsdon gave her familiarity with the palatial estates of the great and with the people who were born to them, she is conscious of her marginal relationship to their world. The valedictory to Cookham is also a valediction to the unusual privileges of her youth. The book of poems she produced in response to that farewell manages at one and the same time to embrace her loss in religious terms, to assert a feminist position in response to arbitrary masculine privilege, and to make a bid for restoration of her place, however peripheral, among the great, through the agency of female patrons.

A beautifully printed and bound copy of *Salve Deus* survives from Prince Henry's library, possibly a gift directly from the Countess of Cumberland, or perhaps reaching the Prince through his master of music and Alphonso's cousin, Nicholas Lanier. Alphonso himself gave a copy as a gift to Thomas Jones, active in Irish politics and Lord Chancellor of Ireland since 1605, whom he probably knew from military service in Ireland.[29] Both of these copies omit many of the dedicatory poems (see Textual Introduction below). There is no evidence that these gifts or any of the dedications produced any patronage for the Lanyers.

Alphonso Lanyer's death in 1613 made Aemilia's life more difficult. The hay and grain patent became the subject of litigation between Aemilia and Alphonso's relatives over the next twenty and more years,[30] and she was forced to try at least one desperate measure to maintain herself and her now-grown son, who was about twenty when Alphonso died.

In 1617 Aemilia Lanyer founded a school in the wealthy suburb of St. Giles in the Field, which she kept until 1619, but her residence was marred by dispute and litigation with the landlord over rent and building repairs. The dispute came to a head in 1620 when she sued her

---

29. See Textual Introduction. The Irish connection is cited in *Kissing the Rod: An Anthology of Seventeenth-Century Women's Verse*, ed. Germaine Greer et al. (New York: Noonday, 1989), 45.

30. S P 14 (James I), 75/22; S P 16 (Charles I), 283/57, 327/128, 356/95, 391/81.

landlord for the recovery of money spent for repairs and for a stay of his suits against her, and he counter-sued, claiming she had left without paying the last quarter's rent, and with the property in bad repair.[31]

St. Giles in the Field was north and slightly east of Charing Cross in the district of Greater London now known as the Seven Dials. Map C (xlv) shows the area to have been mostly rural, and near the main roads to Uxbridge and Reading to the northwest and west. What Lanyer had sought to rent was a farmhouse without two of its outbuildings, and she accuses the landlord, an attorney named Edward Smith, of setting up a lease he could break when he found a better tenant who would also rent the two outbuildings and whom he deemed more reliable. Through the legal diction of the petition to Chancery Court we perhaps catch a glimpse of her voice:

> November 1620 ... To the Right Honorable Francis Lorde Verulam Lord Chauncelor of England. In most humble mannor complanynge sheweth unto your good Lordshipp your Lordships Oratrix Emelia Lanier widdow late wife of captayne Alfonsoe Lanyer his ma[jes]ties servante deceased. That the said Oratrix by the death of the said husband beinge left in verry poore estate hee havinge spente a greate parte of his estate in the servinge of the Late Queene in her warres of Ireland and other places she proposes said Oratrix for her maynetaynaunce and releefe was compelled to teach and educate the children of divers persons of worth and understandinge That one Edward Smith of the middle Temple counsellor of the Law was posessed of the lease of a house in St. Giles ... which she thought was fitt for the purpose. She repaired unto the said Edward Smith about August 1617 and did agree with him to take a lease of said house with all the appurtenaunces whatsoever except one stable and haylofte belonging.

They made an agreement, according to Lanyer, that rent of £22 per year would be paid quarterly, but the exact timing and method was another subject of dispute. Lanyer complains that the terms of the agreement were deliberately hedged in Smith's favor, though she admits she let him draw them up. Her explanation, if true, adds more com-

---

31. PRO Chancery Case, C2/ James I L11/64.

plexity to her character: "And because said Edward Smith was a counselor at law and professed much friendshipe and kindenes unto the said Oratrix she was content to referre the drawinge of the said lease unto the said Edward Smith. But contrary to the said trust imposed in him by the said Oratrix [he] would not draw such indenture and lease but did seale and deliver a note in writing which hee tould her was a good lease and such … as was agreed. hee had made the same only for his owne Advantage and contrary to the saide Agreement." Lanyer then claims that Smith found "a better Tennaunte who would give him more rente and take the stables and haylofte," and began to harrass her about repairs and the due dates of her rent.

Lanyer's petition concludes by claiming that "said Edward Smith is still indebted to her for the some of ten pounds and upwards for repairs" and requesting "his said Majesties gratious writt of injunction to see directed to the said Edward Smith his councillors attourneyes and solicitors for the staye of all suits of common law" until she can receive a hearing in the chancery court. In his response, Smith acknowledges that he found a better tenant, Sir Edward Morgan, but presses his rent and repair grievances against Aemilia all the same. This dispute, too, fades from view. We have no idea what Lanyer taught during the two years she kept the school, nor whom she taught. The episode shows that she was enterprising and had strength of character, and (as in the disputes over Alphonso's patent) she was not intimidated by the legal system.

The few remaining glimpses of Lanyer's life suggest that she spent her later years with or around her son's family. If they were not wealthy, neither were they poor. Henry Lanyer had joined the family trade and become a court musician, a flautist. He married Joyce Mansfield on 18 August 1623, at the London Church of St. Andrew by the Wardrobe, in the London ward of Baynard's Castle. Henry and Joyce bore a daughter, Mary, christened 25 July 1627, and a son, Henry, christened 16 January 1630, both at St. James, Clerkenwell, in whose parish the family had settled.[32] This suburban parish was slightly north and about halfway

---

32. IGI, Greater London.

between St. Giles in the Field and St. Botolph's Bishopsgate, closer to the walls of the City than St. Giles or Westminster had been (see Map D, xlvi). In the early seventeenth century the parish seems to have been reasonably prosperous; it counted Thomas Chaloner, tutor to Prince Henry, among the church vestrymen, and was responsible for maintaining one of the finest fresh water wells in the Greater London area.[33]

Henry died in October 1633, at the age of forty. His will was proved in the Archdeaconry Court of London in November, leaving care for his minor children with his wife, Joyce, to whom they were formally granted in 1634.[34] Baptista Bassano had been equally careful to make sure the mother of his child had legal custody and responsibility. Aemilia apparently had a role in helping to raise her grandchildren, Mary and Henry; as she continued negotiations and litigations with her in-laws over Alphonso's patent through the 1630's, she did so on behalf of her grandchildren as well as herself.

Aemilia Bassano Lanyer was buried on 3 April 1645, at St. James, Clerkenwell.[35] The parish record lists her as a "pensioner," a term which designated a steady income. Her seventy-six years had seen all of the reign of King James I (1603–25) as well as most of the reigns of Queen Elizabeth (1558–1603) and King Charles I (1625–49).

Salve Deus Rex Judæorum

Salve Deus Rex Judæorum's official publication date, 1611, was also the publication year of the King James Bible, John Donne's *Anatomy of the World*, quartos of three Shakespeare plays, one Jonson play, a reprint of

---

33. Greater London Record Office, Miscellaneous Vestry Records from St. James, Clerkenwell, P76.JS.7 140.

34. Guildhall Library 9050/6 (1633 Reg. 6, 134ᵛ; 1634 Reg. 6, 145).

35. *A True Register of all the Chr[is]teninges, Mariages, and Burialles in the Parishe of St. James, Clarkenwell, from the yeare of our Lorde God 1551*, ed. Robert Hovenden (London: Harleian Soc., 1891), 210 (Henry Lanyer) and 263 (Aemilia Lanyer).

Marlowe's *Faustus*, Chapman's translation of Homer, and the first collected edition of Edmund Spenser's *Works*. Lanyer's volume is an attractive quarto printed by Valentine Simmes and sold by Richard Bonian, respectable members of their trades. The book's only acknowledgement of masculine authority is the title page's description of Lanyer as "Wife to Captain Alfonso Lanyer Servant to the Kings Majestie." Beyond that, the book is dedicated and addressed only to women, assumes a community of intellectual women, and makes no serious apology for a woman poet publishing her own work.

This unapologetic creation of a community of good women for whom another woman is the spokesperson and commemorator is unusual and possibly unique in early seventeenth-century England. During the sixteenth century Englishwomen found voices through the contradictory injunctions of Protestantism, which on the one hand reasserted the traditional expectation of womanly silence and subservience, but on the other hand affirmed the supremacy of individual conscience, even in women, to whom God could speak directly and, in theory, allow exceptions to the general rule of silence. So the very popular Protestant tract, *A Godlie Forme of Householde Government* (1598), allows a wife some authority over children and servants but demands full obedience to her husband, to whom she must be "dutifull, faithfull, and loving," and silent if she disagrees with him.[36] Yet women were increasingly free to translate religious works and write of their own religious experience, even to the extent of producing religious verse.[37] The certification of her husband's name on the title page, then, gives Lanyer authority to speak outside the household, and her religious topic is not on the surface exceptionable.

---

36. Robert Cleaver and John Dod, *A Godlie Forme of Householde Government* (London, 1598; eight editions to 1630), F3ᵛ–F4, 1612 ed.

37. See Margaret P. Hannay, ed., *Silent But for the Word: Tudor Women as Patrons, Translators, and Writers of Religious Works* (Kent, Ohio: Kent State Univ. Press, 1985), especially Hannay's introduction and the essays by John N. King on Catherine Parr, Elaine V. Beilin on Anne Askew, Carole Levin on Lady Jane Grey, Beth Wynne Fiskin on Mary Sidney's Psalms, and Gary Waller's summary essay, "Struggling into Discourse: The Emergence of Renaissance Women's Writing," 238–56.

Nevertheless the *Salve Deus* is very different from its predecessors. Although Mary Sidney, Countess of Pembroke, had written in praise of Queen Elizabeth, and a great many male poets had dedicated work to the Queen and such important patronesses as the Countess of Pembroke and Lucy, Countess of Bedford, there is no comparable work of sustained and exclusive dedication to women patrons. Further, the central poem, the "Salve Deus" itself, has no generic predecessor among English women's writing. The first identifiable woman religious poet writing in English was probably Anne Lok (Prowse), who appended a poetic meditation on the fifty-first psalm to her translation (from the French) of Calvin's *Sermons upon the Songe that Ezechias made after he had bene sicke* (1560).[38] The most visible Elizabethan woman poet is certainly the Countess of Pembroke, with her 107 psalms completing the sequence begun by her brother, Sir Philip Sidney. The Countess's complex and sophisticated lyric versions of psalms 44–150 were widely circulated in manuscript and admired by Donne and Jonson, as well as Lanyer (see "The Authors Dream," 27, lines 117–24). Apart from these English psalm translations, there is one other notable work of religious verse before Lanyer: Elizabeth Melvill, Lady Culros, published *Ane Godlie Dreame* in Edinburgh in 1606. A dream allegory that breaks the commitment to "translation" that previously had characterized English women's verse, it nonetheless sidesteps the issue of authority by situating the poem in the relationship between God and the individual conscience. By contrast, Lanyer's religious poem claims biblical and historical authority and grants the viewpoint of women as much or greater authenticity as that of men.

The dedicatory poems situate Lanyer among the increasing number of professional poets who sought support through patronage. It was still usual for high-born writers to avoid the self-advertising "stigma of

---

38. There is some dispute over whether the verses are hers, since she claims they were given to her by a "friend," but most scholars of the work find the style fully compatible with Lok's translation, and the "friend" a common version of the humilitas *topos*. See Susanne Woods, "The Body Penitent: A 1560 Calvinist Sonnet Sequence," *ANQ* 5 (1992): 137–40.

print," but it was acceptable for middle-class writers to claim attention—and assistance—by blazoning their patrons' virtues in verse. The patronage system was an early step in the professionalization of literature, but its economic impetus received social and intellectual force by claiming to reflect classical models and ideals. The classical epideictic tradition saw the poetry of praise as a means of affirming social and cultural values. Renaissance poets invoked that tradition and used it to valorize their own role as definers of, as well as speakers for, their society.[39]

It was usual for the lower born poet to acknowledge ritual unworthiness in speaking to social superiors, and to request and at the same time claim the forgiveness that sends the grace of worthiness to the poet from the exalted subject of the verse. By acknowledging social distance, the poet bridges it, and by acknowledging humility, the poet receives the grace of excellence. This is precisely what Lanyer does in her dedicatory verses, though her stance is complicated by her status as a woman as well as a commoner. It leads her to claim a special identity with her dedicatees, and to allow their dignity and high birth to assert the diginity and merit of all women. By collapsing her unworthiness as a woman into the general unworthiness all poets must acknowledge in their dedications to the high born, she renders the happenstance of gender as visible as, and as ultimately inconsequential as, the male poet's happenstance of birth.

The prefatory poems are all dedications, beginning with poems to three royals: Queen Anne, her daughter Princess Elizabeth, and Lady Arbella Stuart (who, as King James's chief rival for the throne, was imprisoned in the Tower of London later that same year). There follow

---

39. Of Lanyer's contemporaries, Ben Jonson was the most audacious in claiming the social role and value of the poet. Among works that offer insight into Jonson's strategies and objectives, see Jonathan Goldberg, *James I and the Politics of Literature* (Baltimore: Johns Hopkins Univ. Press, 1983), 17–18 and 120–23; Richard Helgerson, *Self-Crowned Laureates: Spenser, Jonson, Milton and the Literary System* (Berkeley and Los Angeles: Univ. California Press, 1983), 168–72; and Stanley Fish, "Authors-Readers: Jonson's Community of the Same," in Stephen Greenblatt, ed., *Representing the English Renaissance* (Berkeley and Los Angeles: Univ. California Press, 1988), 231–63.

poems to Susan, Countess Dowager of Kent; Mary [Sidney], Countess Dowager of Pembroke; Lucy, Countess of Bedford; a prose dedication to Lanyer's chief patron, Margaret, Countess Dowager of Cumberland; verse again for Katherine, Countess of Suffolk and for Margaret's daughter Anne [Clifford], Countess of Dorset; and finally a prose preface "To the Vertuous Reader." The "Salve Deus" poem is framed by dedicatory praise of Margaret of Cumberland, and the concluding "Cooke-ham" is written for her and her daughter Anne.

These dedications provide Lanyer's principal authority for publishing her verse. Her central topic, Christ's Passion, provides another authority. If women are not expected to write, they are expected to experience the joy and power of conversion and cannot be enjoined from expressing what God has spoken to them. Lanyer claims that her full conversion to Christ resulted from the influence of her main dedicatee, the Countess Dowager of Cumberland, and that other women, including the Countess Dowager of Kent (in whose household she had resided as an unrepentant young woman), Queen Anne (through her godly example), and the Countess of Pembroke (through her psalms), had godly influences on her.

The title poem on Christ's Passion is a truly original work. For an Englishwoman to write authoritatively on so sacred a subject is unusual in itself, but for her to revise fifteen hundred years of traditional commentary in the process is unheard of. A useful contrast is between Lanyer's "Salve Deus" and Queen Katherine Parr's *The Lamentacion of a Sinner* (1547). The latter includes some commentary on Biblical texts, arguing a Protestant position on justification by faith among other things, but makes no challenge to the primacy of men.[40] As one critic has noted, Parr's work can be read as a woman's work more by what it leaves out than what it puts in: "Femininity circum-

---

40. See commentary by John King and quotations from Parr in King's "Influence of Catherine Parr," in Hannay, ed., *Silent But for the Word*, 50–51, and Elaine V. Beilin, *Redeeming Eve: Women Writers of the English Renaissance* (Princeton: Princeton Univ. Press, 1987), 72–74.

scribes the public domain within Parr's discourse and screens topicality, polemic, and personality from the text."[41]

By contrast, the "Salve Deus" starts with personal references and has a strong polemical thrust, attacking the vanity and blindness of men and justifying women's right to be free of masculine subjugation. Many of the arguments are put in the voice of Pilate's wife, whom the Bible reports as warning her husband to have "nothing to do with that just man," Jesus (Mat. 27:19). Lanyer expands that brief (and ignored) warning into a lengthy "apologie," or defense and explanation, for Eve, and moves so seamlessly from the argument back to the narrative that it is difficult to tell where the voice of Pilate's wife is meant to end and the voice of the narrator continue.

The "Salve Deus" begins with a short tribute to the late Queen Elizabeth I and moves to a lengthy and meditative dedication of the work to the Countess Dowager of Cumberland. Lanyer acknowledges that this poem is not "Those praisefull lines of that delightful place, / Which you commaunded me," presumably the celebration of Cookham, but is instead a praise of Christ's "almightie love," which comforts the worthy Countess in her unhappiness. The references to unhappiness are presumably to Margaret's alienation from her late husband, George Clifford, third Earl of Cumberland, and the legal battles with his relatives that followed his death in 1605. The Countess championed the claims of her daughter, and Cumberland's only heir, Anne Clifford, but King James and the court bureaucracy were willing only to negotiate cash settlements that were well short of Anne's full legal claim to the various Cumberland lands and titles.[42] These both Margaret and Anne refused to accept, assuring the alienation and suffering that Lanyer

---

41. Janel Mueller, "A Tudor Queen Finds Voice: Katherine Parr's *Lamentation of a Sinner*," in *The Historical Renaissance*, ed. Heather Dubrow and Richard Strier (Chicago: Univ. Chicago Press, 1988), 42.

42. See Barbara Lewalski's summary of this story and Lanyer's relationship to it, in "Rewriting Patriarchy and Patronage: Margaret Clifford, Anne Clifford, and Aemilia Lanyer," *The Yearbook of English Studies* 21 (1991): 87–106.

chronicles in this poem and "Cooke-ham." Lanyer offers Margaret the story of Christ's Passion as a comfort and assurance of God's love in the face of these worldly tribulations.

The version of the Passion Lanyer describes follows closely Matthew 26:30–28:10, the only version which contains the warning of Pilate's wife. She also borrows freely from other gospels, taking references to women wherever they appear. (See Mark 14:26–16:11, Luke 22:39–24:12, and John 18:1–20:18.) The best preparation for reading Lanyer's poem is to read the stories in Matthew and Luke, though Lanyer's version is different from theirs in being uniquely woman-centered throughout, chronicling female virtues and suffering as part of the poet's strategy for comforting and praising the Countess of Cumberland. Within that context, however, the story is a richly imagined version of the most central events of the Christian faith.

The Passion, or suffering, of Jesus Christ refers to the last events of his life and is the story that brings into vivid focus the basic elements of Christian theology, which Lanyer's version assumes throughout. According to that theology, God created humans to enjoy peaceful and productive lives on earth, in harmony with all creation. Humankind (represented by Adam and Eve) in turn pledged obedience to God, symbolized by following the injunction against eating from the tree of knowledge of good and evil in the Garden of Eden. Disobedience and the fall from God's grace occurred when Satan took the form of a serpent to tempt Eve into eating from the forbidden tree, and she in turn gave the fruit to Adam, who chose to eat it even though he was fully aware of the consequences. Eve's lesser knowledge and Adam's knowing acceptance of disobedience were key points for those Renaissance writers who sought to defend women against the common charge that they were responsible for the fall of humankind.[43] Lanyer, in the "Eves

---

43. See Linda Woodbridge, *Women and the English Renaissance: Literature and the Nature of Womankind 1540–1620* (Urbana and Chicago: Univ. Illinois Press, 1984), 39–40, 70, 90, and passim; and Katherine Usher Henderson and Barbara F. McManus, *Half Humankind: Contexts and Texts of the Controversy about Women in England, 1540–1640* (Urbana and Chicago: Univ. Illinois Press, 1985), 7, 13, and passim.

Apologie" section (lines 761–832), uses this argument and extends it, concluding that male culpability in the death of Christ far outweighs Eve's tragic misunderstanding: "If one weake woman simply did offend, / This sinne of yours, hath no excuse, nor end" (lines 831–32).

Separation from God became the inherited condition called sin, which in turn prompted people to create a world of misery. Jesus, as the Christ and God incarnate, took on all the sufferings of humanity, canceled original sin by his death, and brought the promise of God's saving grace through his resurrection. According to Christian theology, then, although sin and suffering remain in the world, God in Christ has promised comfort, hope, and eternal life, and at the end of time the world itself will be transformed. Lanyer's repeated references to the Countess of Cumberland's suffering and the comfort she receives from Christ draw upon these theological assumptions.

Lanyer retells the powerful story of Jesus' last night and day, meditating and expanding on the events from a female point of view. The story proper begins at line 329, but Jesus' first action appears in line 333, when he "to Mount Olives went, though sore afraid." In Renaissance numerology 333 is a figure for the trinitarian God, and a version of the number nine, a number thought to express God's self-contained perfection. Although Lanyer does not appear to work numerology into the poem throughout, as some of her contemporaries apparently did (Spenser's *Epithalamion* is a famous example), it is possible that her choosing to begin the action at this line is significant.

As the poem proceeds, digressions focusing on women interweave the story. These include "Eves Apologie" (lines 761–832); "The teares of the daughters of Jerusalem" (lines 969–1008); "The sorrow of the virgin Marie" (lines 1009–40); the story of Mary's annunciation and an assertion of her centrality to redemption (lines 1033–1136); and the Countess's piety (lines 1169–70, and throughout). The last third of the poem is a meditation on the relationship between the Christian soul, specifically represented by the Countess, and the crucified and risen Christ.

In lines 1297–1320 Lanyer turns the reader's gaze on the body of the risen Christ, described in the sensuous language of the "Song of Songs," or *Book of Canticles:*

> His lips like skarlet threeds, yet much more sweet
> Than is the sweetest hony dropping dew,
> Or hony combes, where all the Bees doe meet;
>
> .   .   .   .
>
> His lips, like Lillies, dropping downe pure mirrhe,
> Whose love, before all worlds we doe preferre.
>
> (lines 1314–16; 1319–20)

The next stanza confirms the Countess as the location for Lanyer's sensuous vision of Christ, and as the ultimate true spouse of that Christ:

> in your heart I leave
> His perfect picture, where it still shall stand,
> Deepely engraved in that holy shrine,
> Environed with Love and Thoughts divine.
>
> (lines 1325–28)

The last 500 lines of the poem interweave the significance of Christ's redemption with praise for the many virtues, particularly heroic faithfulness, that the Countess embodies. The dedicatory language at the beginning of the poem had catalogued the weaknesses of outward beauty in contrast to the Countess's inner virtue; this last section catalogues Biblical heroines and other symbols of purity and faithfulness and finds the Countess even worthier of praise than they. In the midst of all this, Lanyer asserts her poetic vocation and portrays herself quite literally as born to praise the great Countess:

> And knowe, when first into this world I came,
> This charge was giv'n me by th'Eternall powres,
> Th'everlasting Trophie of thy fame,
> To build and decke it with the sweetest flowres
> That virtue yeelds.
>
> (lines 1457–61)

The catalogue concludes with an extensive comparison between the Countess and the Queen of Sheba, who sought the wisdom of

Solomon. Folded in with the comparison are a vision of the apocalypse (lines 1649–72) and a baroque description of the blood of Christ:

> Sweet holy rivers, pure celestiall springs,
> Proceeding from the fountaine of our life;
> Sweet sugred currents that salvation brings,
> Cleare christall streames, purging all sinne and strife,
> Faire floods, where soules do bathe their snow-white wings,
> Before they flie to true eternall life:
>> Sweet Nectar and Ambrosia, food of Saints,
>> Which whoso tasteth, never after faints.
>
> This hony dropping dew of holy love,
> Sweet milke, wherewith we weaklings are restored.   (lines 1729–38)

Lanyer's extended transformation of the image of Christ's blood is not characteristic of Jacobean poetics, but is an early indicator of a richly sensuous biblical poetics that we usually associate with that later master of baroque religious imagery, Richard Crashaw. While they have little else in common, both poets spent their lives surrounded by music.

The 1610/1 publication of "The Description of Cooke-ham" pre-dates by five years the poem usually cited as founding a tradition of country house poems in seventeenth-century England, Ben Jonson's "To Penshurst."[44] Editors usually assume that Jonson's poem was written sometime before late 1612, since a reference to "King James ... With his brave sonne, the Prince" (lines 76–77) is generally taken to refer to the King in company with Prince Henry, who died in November of that year.[45] It is remotely possible that "To Penshurst"

---

44. G. R. Hibbard, "The Country House Poem of the Seventeenth Century," *Journal of the Warburg and Courtauld Institutes* 19 (1956): 159–74, outlined the tradition and made the claim for "To Penshurst." His assumptions have been largely followed by subsequent editors and critics, notably William B. Hunter, *The Complete Poetry of Ben Jonson* (New York: Doubleday, 1963; rpt. Norton, 1968), 75; Raymond Williams, *The Country and the City* (New York: Oxford Univ. Press, 1973), 27–34; and William A. McClung, *The Country House in English Renaissance Poetry* (Berkeley: Univ. California Press, 1977).

45. E.g., Hunter, 80, n. 23, and George Parfitt, ed., *Ben Jonson: The Complete Poems* (Baltimore: Penguin, 1975), 508.

was written before "A Description of Cooke-ham," but Lanyer's work is without question the first in print. Jonson's poem first appeared as the second poem in the "Forrest" section of his *Works* (1616).

Lanyer's poem shows some evidence that she was aware of country house poems by Horace and Martial, and that she is writing in the Augustan tradition of contrasting an idyllic natural order with a fallen human civilization—themes which Jonson, Thomas Carew, Robert Herrick, and Andrew Marvell variously exploit in their later reflections of classical models.[46] More to the point, however, is the poem's exploitation of the natural order as a mirror of human feeling, a device firmly grounded in the pastoral tradition and its English representations.[47] The conclusion of "Cooke-ham" implies that the poem was commissioned by the Countess of Cumberland ("Wherein I have perform'd her noble hest," line 207), and therefore asserts itself as a professional work in a long-standing tradition of poet as memorializer of great places, persons, and deeds. Cookham's epithet, "that delightfull Place" (line 32), recalls both the classical *locus amoenus* or "delightful place" and the Christian Eden, both worlds in which the natural order reflects social and spiritual harmony. But the imperfection of the larger world, signified by "fortune" and "occasions," conspires to send the Countess, Anne, and the poet away from the place and from each other. The poet loses the rich companionship of her social superiors, but in the process she creates a poem that eternizes the place and its former inhabitants, including the poet herself. Despite the poem's melancholy topic, it therefore concludes the volume with an unmistakable

---

46. See Barbara K. Lewalski, "The Lady of the Country-House Poem," in *The Fashioning and Functioning of the British Country House*, ed. Gervase Jackson-Stops, Gordon J. Schochet, Lena Cowen Orlin, and Elisabeth Blair MacDougall (Studies in the History of Art, no. 25. Hanover and London: National Gallery of Art, 1989), 261–75, for the relation of "Cooke-ham" to its tradition.

47. Spenser's *Shepheardes Calendar* (1579) is a notable and popular example. As a literate person around Queen Elizabeth's court in the late 1580s and early 1590s, Lanyer very probably knew Spenser's work. The first edition of Spenser's *Faerie Queene* (1590) includes a dedicatory sonnet to Henry, Lord Hunsdon, presumably written during the time when Aemilia Bassano was Hunsdon's mistress.

claim for the poet's classical role as a participant in the social order she celebrates.

A short prose note "To the doubtfull Reader" provides a coda to the whole volume. In it Lanyer assures us that the volume's title, *Salve Deus Rex Judæorum*, came to her in a dream "many yeares before I had any intent to write" the story of the Passion of Christ. She considers this dream "a significant token, that I was appointed to performe this Worke." A generation before Milton, Aemilia Lanyer thus professes herself to be God's poet.

Selected Bibliography

Beilin, Elaine V. "The Feminization of Praise: Aemilia Lanyer." *Redeeming Eve: Women Writers of the English Renaissance*. Princeton: Princeton Univ. Press, 1987.

Lewalski, Barbara K. "Of God and Good Women: The Poems of Aemilia Lanyer." In *Silent but for the Word: Tudor Women as Patrons, Translators, and Writers of Religious Works*, edited by Margaret P. Hannay, 203–24. Kent, Ohio: Kent State Univ. Press, 1985.

———. "The Lady of the Country-House Poem." In *The Fashioning and Functioning of the British Country House*, edited by Gervase Jackson-Stops, Gordon J. Schochet, Lena Cowen Orlin, and Elisabeth Blair MacDougall, 261–75. Studies in the History of Art, no. 25. Hanover and London: National Gallery of Art, 1989.

———. "Re-writing Patriarchy and Patronage: Margaret Clifford, Anne Clifford, and Aemilia Lanyer." *The Yearbook of English Studies* 21 (1991): 87–106.

———. "Imagining Female Community: Aemilia Lanyer's Poems." *Writing Women in Jacobean England*. Cambridge: Harvard Univ. Press, 1993.

McGrath, Lynette. "'Let Us Have Our Libertie Againe': Amelia Lanier's Seventeenth-Century Feminist Voice," *Women's Studies* 20 (1992): 331–48.

———. "Metaphoric Subversions: Feasts and Mirrors in Amelia Lanier's *Salve Deus Rex Judaeorum*," *LIT*, 3 (1991): 101–13.

Mueller, Janel. "The Feminist Poetics of Aemilia Lanyer's 'Salve Deus Rex Judaeorum,'" in *Feminist Measures: Soundings in Poetry and Theory*, edited by Lynn Keller and Cristianne Miller. Ann Arbor: Univ. of Michigan Press, 1993.

Rowse, A. L. *Simon Forman: Sex and Society in Shakespeare's Age*. London: Weidenfeld & Nicolson, 1974.

———. *The Poems of Shakespeare's Dark Lady*. London: Jonathan Cape, 1978.

Wall, Wendy. "Our Bodies/Our Texts?: Renaissance Women and the Trials of Authorship." In *Anxious Power: Reading, Writing and Ambivalence in Narrative by Women,* edited by Carol J. Singley and Susan Elizabeth Sweeney, 51–71. Series in Feminist Criticism and Theory. Albany: State Univ. of New York Press, 1993.

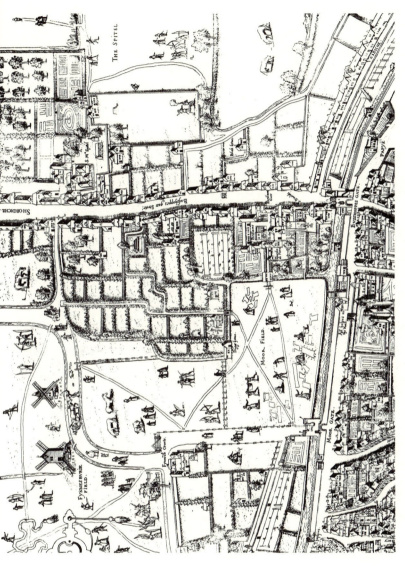

MAP A: AREA OF ST. BOTOLPH'S, BISHOPSGATE, C. 1562 (the "Agas" Map, Guildhall Library).

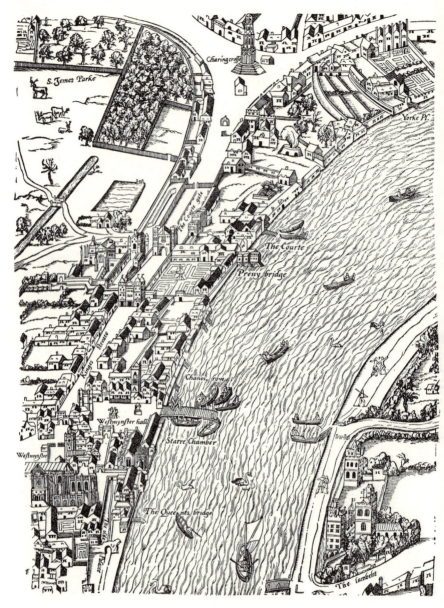

MAP B: WESTMINSTER, c. 1559,
with Longditch area to the left middle and St. Margaret's church just above
Westminster Abbey, lower left (The Copperplate Map, Museum of London).

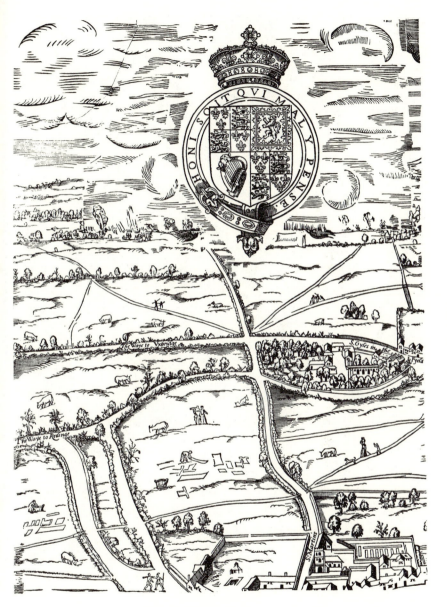

MAP C: ST. GILES IN THE FIELDS, C. 1559
(The Copperplate Map, Museum of London).

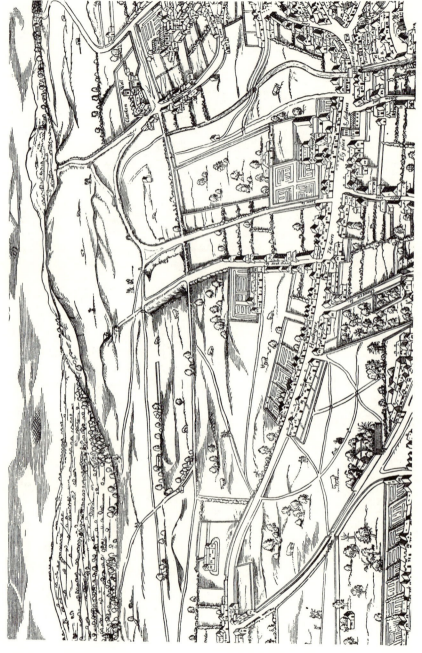

MAP D: ST. JAMES, CLERKENWELL, UPPER RIGHT, C. 1562, Lanyer's burial site (The "Agas" Map, Guildhall Library).

TEXTUAL INTRODUCTION

Aemilia Lanyer's *Salve Deus Rex Judæorum* is a quarto volume entered into the Stationers' Register 2 October 1610, and probably published shortly thereafter, although it is dated 1611 on the title page.[1] There are nine known copies, more than twice as many as were thought to be extant when Pollard and Redgrave compiled the first edition of the *Short Title Catalogue of Books Printed in English to 1640* (the STC), which lists four copies.[2]

Five of the nine copies are complete or virtually so: two at the Huntington Library, two at the Folger Library, and one at the Avon County Library in Bath. These copies have poems and prose dedications from a3ʳ through f3ᵛ, in the following order: "To the Queenes most Excellent Majestie" (a3ʳ–b1ᵛ); "To the Lady Elizabeths Grace" (b2ʳ, with b2ᵛ blank); "To all vertuous Ladies in generall" (b3ʳ–b4ᵛ); "To the Ladie Arabella" (c1ʳ, with c1ᵛ blank); "To the Ladie Susan, Countesse Dowager of Kent, and Daughter to the Duchesse of Suffolke" (c2ʳ–c2ᵛ); "The Authors Dreame to the Ladie Marie, the Countesse Dowager of Pembrooke" (c3ʳ–d3ᵛ); "To the Ladie Lucie, Countesse of Bedford" (d4ʳ–d4ᵛ); "To the Ladie Margaret Countesse Dowager of Cumberland" (e1ʳ–e1ᵛ; in prose); "To the Ladie Katherine Countesse of Suffolke" (e2ʳ–e3ᵛ); "To the Ladie Anne, Countesse of Dorcet" (e4ʳ–f2ʳ, with f2ᵛ blank); "To the Vertuous Reader" (f3ʳ–f3ᵛ; in prose). All but one of these copies has a blank leaf at f4ʳ–f4ᵛ. There follows the "Salve Deus" poem, from A1ʳ–H1ᵛ, "The Description of Cooke-ham" from H2ʳ–I1ʳ, and the short prose explanation of the volume's title, "To the doubtfull Reader," on I1ᵛ. The Bath Library copy is missing leaf I1.

---

1. The Chapin Library copy in Williamstown, Massachusetts, has an inscription on its title page dating it as a gift of Alphonso Lanyer, 8 November 1610; see below.

2. The revised STC lists eight copies: one copy of an issue with a four-line printer's imprint on the title page (STC 15227) and seven of a presumably later variant with a five-line imprint (STC 15227.5). The Folger Shakespeare Library holds two of the five-line imprint copies rather than the one copy listed in the STC.

The four remaining copies are missing substantial portions of the volume. At least two of these, at the Victoria and Albert Museum and the Chapin Library in Williamstown, Massachusetts, intentionally omit some of the dedicatory verses. The Victoria and Albert copy is a presentation copy to Prince Henry, King James's oldest son, and is beautifully printed and bound with the Prince's coat of arms on the cover.[3] This is a small quarto bound in vellum with gilt borders and devices on the four corners and the encircled ostrich feather emblem of Prince Henry, also in gilt, in the center of the front and back bindings. There are holes for (absent) ribbons in the front and back, and gilt devices and lines on the spine. The recto of the page preceding the title page has "Cumberland" in ink at the very edge, center top. The margins are wide, the paper clean, and the inking and impress of printing particularly clear.

It has only the dedications to the Queen, Lady Elizabeth, "To all vertuous Ladies," to Lucie of Bedford, Margaret of Cumberland, Anne of Dorset, and "To the Vertuous Reader." Omitted are the poems to Lady Arabella, Susan of Kent, the Countess of Pembroke, and Katherine of Suffolk. Certainly Prince Henry's cousin, Arbella Stuart, was out of favor, and presumably Lanyer had reason to omit the others from some copies as well. This book may have reached Prince Henry through Margaret, Countess of Cumberland, as Barbara Lewalski argues from the title page signature. Another possibility would be through Nicholas Lanier, Henry's master of music, who was Alphonso's cousin. Alexander Dyce owned this copy in the nineteenth century, and tipped in the missing leaves from another copy. (See xlix, n. 4.)

The Chapin Library copy at Williams College omits the same poems, and also drops the poem to Lucie, Countess of Bedford, and the prose dedication "To the Vertuous Reader." The shortest version of all, this copy therefore has only (in order): the dedicatory poems to Queen Anne, Princess Elizabeth, "To all vertuous Ladies," the prose piece to the Countess of Cumberland, and the poem to her daughter Anne; the "Salve Deus"; and "Cooke-ham." Written on the title page

3. Victoria and Albert Library, shelfmark 5675 8.L.20.

in a contemporary hand is "guift of Mr. Alfonso Lanyer" followed by ".8.No 1610," and then the signature "Tho: Jones." Alphonso Lanyer had served in Ireland with Thomas Jones, who was Archbishop of Dublin in 1610. D4 was probably lost when D1–3 were removed, but in any case the direct feminist prose of "To the Vertuous Reader" was unlikely to appeal to Jones. The prose piece may have been kept in the volume to Prince Henry out of respect for his reputation as an intellectual who was more likely to enjoy its wit, or it may be that Prince Henry's volume was one of several originally given to Margaret, Countess of Cumberland, as Lewalski suggests.

The British Library copy also lacks many of the dedicatory verses. Now in a 1929 British Museum binding, this is probably the copy that Dyce described as "imperfect,"[4] and from which he took the nine leaves that his own copy lacked. All those leaves are missing from the BL copy,

---

4. In a letter to fellow antiquarian Edward Bliss now bound with the Bindley/Rice copy in the Huntington Library, HN 62139 (the copy from which this volume was prepared): "My copy of Mrs. Lanyer's poem (which was Prince Henry's) is *now* complete: I made it up from another (imperfect) copy ... It originally wanted *nine leaves* of the Dedicatory Poems, which appeared (from the fine state of the book) to have been *purposely omitted in that copy.* The leaves in question were—Sigs. c, c2, c3, c4, d, d2, d3,—e2, e3.—The matter contained in the above mentioned leaves is—'To the Ladie Arabella' 'To the Ladie Susan, Countesse Dowager of Kent,' &c. 'The Author's Dreame, to the Ladie Marie, the Countesse Dowager of Pembrooke.' 'To the Ladie Katherine Countesse of Suffolke.' The British Library copy shelfmark is c.71.h.15. 5 a–f4, A–H4, I2 (Ai, f4 and Iii, are blank leaves)." A commentary by "e.c.e." in the Bodleian copy offers a somewhat misleading piece of bibliography: "The introductory leaves appear to have been added as an afterthought, and Heber's, which was an early presentation copy to a friend, lacked them. Twelve of them are deficient in the British Museum copy, and Prince Henry's copy, afterwards in the Dyce collection, had them inserted from another copy. ... on fol. 9 (sig.ci) the author has addressed a poem to LADY ARABELLA STUART. This leaf is wanting in nearly all known copies, but has been preserved in this one, and is the subject of a letter, the original of which has been bound with this copy at the end, from ISAAC D'ISRAELI to G. Wright, Esq., of Leeds, a previous owner of the copy." The note also points out that D'Israeli (1766–1844) considered the poem proof of Arbella's reputation as "a learned lady," support for the several pages he devoted to her in his *Curiosities of Literature.* The commentator concludes "This copy ends on G4, and lacks H4–I2, the six leaves which contain the description of Cookham, but the rare preliminary leaves including the sonnet to Lady Arabella Stuart have been preserved, as has been the blank leaf, sig. f4." The notes are concluded: "York, Sep. 1933, e.c.e." In fact, the absence of "Cooke-ham" is more rare than the presence of the "preliminary leaves."

and the size of the remaining preliminary leaves is consistent with the nine leaves tipped into the Dyce copy. Also missing from the BL copy is quire f, containing all but the first seven verses of the poem to Anne of Dorset (f1^r–2^r), "To the Vertuous Reader" (f3^r–3^v), and blank f4.

The fourth incomplete copy, at the Bodleian Library, contains all of the dedicatory material, but is missing its final section, "The Description of Cooke-ham" and "To the doubtfull Reader" (H2^r–Ii^r). It is difficult to make much of this omission.

Poets in this period did sometimes write multiple dedications and target them to potential patrons.[5] If the Chapin and Prince Henry copies were produced near the same time, in late 1610, then it may be that Lanyer first had compiled shorter volumes for various dedicatees, then the more complete volume destined for 1611, and possibly a wider market. There are two known versions of the printer's imprint on the title page, but neither suggests a more particular market than the other. The five-line version of STC 15227.5 simply makes the location of the bookseller more specific.

The Huntington Library copy of STC 15227 (HN 62140), the only one extant, offers this information in the four-line imprint:

At London
Printed by *Valentine Simmes* for *Richard Bonian*, and
are to be sold at his Shop in Paules Churchyard. Anno 1611.

A bibliographical note in the copy says this "was Sir Francis Freeling's and afterwards Halliwell's copy." All the rest of the extant copies (STC 15227.5) have the more specific five-line imprint:

At London
Printed by *Valentine Simmes* for *Richard Bonian*,
and are to be sold at his Shop in Paules Churchyard, at the
Signe of the Floure de Luce and
Crowne. 1611.

---

5. Muriel C. Bradbrook cites the common practice of expecting £2 per dedication, in "Review of *The Paradise of Women*, ed. Betty Travitsky," *Tulsa Studies in Women's Literature*, 2 (Spring 1982): 92.

The title page in all copies is identical except for this.

Composition for this volume was done from a photocopy of the Huntington Library copy, HN 62139, used by permission. It is a fine copy with wide margins and is textually complete.

Note on the Text

This text of the *Salve Deus Rex Judæorum* reproduces the original spelling and punctuation with the following exceptions: the use of *i, j, u, v,* and *w* has been regularized to conform to modern usage. I have silently emended obvious typographical errors, including turned letters (such as *n* for *u*) and spacing errors.

Folger Shakespeare Library copy 1 has some evidence of ink correction of typographical errors, most clearly in "Salve Deus," the change from "oughr" to "ought."

The following further emendations have been made in the text:

"To the Ladie Susan," line 37: "Receive"; copytext "Reccive" (could be "Receive" in Folger copy 1 but is certainly "Reccive" in Folger copy 2)

"The Author's Dream," line 71: "Ladies"; copytext "Ladied"

"To the Ladie Margaret," line 27: "inestimable"; copytext "inestinable"

"To the Ladie Katherine," line 91: "pietie"; copytext "pictie"

"To the Ladie Anne," line 135: "worldly"; copytext "wordly"

"Salve Deus," line 728: "your"; copytext "yout"

   line 782: "ought"; copytext "oughr" (see above)

   line 977: "one"; copytext "on"

   line 1194: "tremble"; copytext "rremble"

   line 1516: "free"; copytext "ftee."

SALVE DEUS
REX JUDÆORUM

Containing,

1 The Passion of Christ.
2 Eves Apologie in defence of Women.
3 The Teares of the Daughters of Jerusalem.
4 The Salutation and Sorrow of the Virgine Marie.

With divers other things not unfit to be read.

Written by Mistris *Æmilia Lanyer*, Wife to Captaine *Alfonso Lanyer* Servant to the Kings Majestie.

A T L O N D O N
Printed by *Valentine Simmes* for *Richard Bonian*, and are to be sold at his Shop in Paules Churchyard, at the Signe of the Floure de Luce and Crowne. 1 6 1 1

SALVE DEUS. An approximation of the layout of the original title page, with the five-line printer's imprint.

To the Queenes most Excellent Majestie

Renowned Empresse, and great Britaines Queene,
Most gratious Mother of succeeding Kings;
Vouchsafe to view that which is seldome seene,
A Womans writing of divinest things:
 Reade it faire Queene, though it defective be, 5
 Your Excellence can grace both It and Mee.

For you have rifled Nature of her store,
And all the Goddesses have dispossest
Of those rich gifts which they enjoy'd before,
But now great Queene, in you they all doe rest. 10
 If now they strived for the golden Ball,
 Paris would give it you before them all.

From *Juno* you have State and Dignities,
From warlike *Pallas*, Wisdome, Fortitude;
And from faire *Venus* all her Excellencies, 15
With their best parts your Highnesse is indu'd:

Title. **Queenes ... Majestie**: Anne of Denmark (1574–1619), Queen to James I and patron of writers and musicians such as Ben Jonson and Henry Lawes.

Line 3. **Vouchsafe**: be willing.

Lines 11–12. **golden ... Paris**: The Trojan shepherd Paris was given possession of a golden ball or apple which the goddess of discord had thrown among the Olympians saying "for the fairest." It was up to Paris to present the ball to one of the three great goddesses, each of whom promised him an appropriate gift: Pallas Athena, wisdom; Hera (Juno), power; Aphrodite (Venus), the most beautiful woman in the world, Helen. (Paris chose Aphrodite, and received his prize.)

Line 16. **indu'd**: endowed.

How much are we to honor those that springs
From such rare beauty, in the blood of Kings?

The Muses doe attend upon your Throne,
With all the Artists at your becke and call;   20
The Sylvane Gods, and Satyres every one,
Before your faire triumphant Chariot fall:
    And shining Cynthia with her nymphs attend
    To honour you, whose Honour hath no end.

From your bright spheare of greatnes where you sit,   25
Reflecting light to all those glorious stars
That wait upon your Throane; To virtue yet
Vouchsafe that splendor which my meannesse bars:
    Be like faire *Phoebe*, who doth love to grace
    The darkest night with her most beauteous face.   30

Apollo's beames doe comfort every creature,
And shines upon the meanest things that be;
Since in Estate and Virtue none is greater,
I humbly wish that yours may light on me:
    That so these rude unpollisht lines of mine,   35
    Graced by you, may seeme the more divine.

Line 19. **Muses**: in Greek myth, nine sisters who represented and bestowed skill in arts and learning, including poetry and music.

Line 21. **Sylvane … Satyres**: pagan creatures of the forest who represent the natural world untamed by art.

Line 23. **Cynthia**: goddess of the moon; also referred to in Lanyer's poems as Phoebe, Diana, Dictina.

Line 28. **meannesse**: humility.   Line 29. **Phoebe**: goddess of the moon.

Line 31. **Apollo**: god of the sun; also referred to in these poems as Phoebus.

Line 33. **Estate**: social and political class.

Looke in this Mirrour of a worthy Mind,
Where some of your faire Virtues will appeare;
Though all it is impossible to find,
Unlesse my Glasse were chrystall, or more cleare: 40
    Which is dym steele, yet full of spotlesse truth,
    And for one looke from your faire eyes it su'th.

Here may your sacred Majestie behold
That mightie Monarch both of heav'n and earth,
He that all Nations of the world controld,   45
Yet tooke our flesh in base and meanest berth:
    Whose daies were spent in poverty and sorrow,
    And yet all Kings their wealth of him do borrow.

For he is Crowne and Crowner of all Kings,
The hopefull haven of the meaner sort,   50
Its he that all our joyfull tidings brings
Of happie raigne within his royall Court:
    Its he that in extremity can give
    Comfort to them that have no time to live.

And since my wealth within his Region stands,   55
And that his Crosse my chiefest comfort is,

Line 37. **Mirrour ... Mind**: that is, the "Salve Deus" poem, which reflects the Queen's virtues.

Line 40. **Glasse**: mirror.

Line 41. **dym steele**: conventionally, a steel mirror gave a truthful reflection. See, for example, George Gascoigne's satire, *The Steele Glas* (1576).

Line 42. **su'th**: sues, begs.   Line 44. **Monarch**: Christ.

Line 46. **meanest berth**: humblest birth.

Line 50. **meaner sort**: lower classes, more humble people.

Line 53. **in extremity**: at the point of death.

Yea in his kingdome onely rests my lands,
Of honour there I hope I shall not misse:
　　Though I on earth doe live unfortunate,
　　Yet there I may attaine a better state.　　　　　60

In the meane time, accept most gratious Queene
This holy worke, Virtue presents to you,
In poore apparell, shaming to be seene,
Or once t'appeare in your judiciall view:
　　But that faire Virtue, though in meane attire,　　65
　　All Princes of the world doe most desire.

And sith all royall virtues are in you,
The Naturall, the Morall, and Divine,
I hope how plaine soever, beeing true,
You will accept even of the meanest line　　　　　70
　　Faire Virtue yeelds; by whose rare gifts you are
　　So highly grac'd, t'exceed the fairest faire.

Behold, great Queene, faire *Eves* Apologie,
Which I have writ in honour of your sexe,
And doe referre unto your Majestie,　　　　　　　75
To judge if it agree not with the Text:
　　And if it doe, why are poore Women blam'd,
　　Or by more faultie Men so much defam'd?

Line 67. **sith:** since.

Line 68. **Naturall ... Divine:** a version of the Scholastic four moral virtues (justice, prudence, temperance, and fortitude) and three divine virtues (faith, hope, and charity).

Line 69. **plaine:** simple, unadorned.　　Line 73. **Apologie:** explanation, defense.

Line 76. **Text:** biblical text.

And this great Lady I have here attired,
In all her richest ornaments of Honour,   80
That you faire Queene, of all the world admired,
May take the more delight to looke upon her:
    For she must entertaine you to this Feast,
    To which your Highnesse is the welcom'st guest.

For here I have prepar'd my Paschal Lambe,   85
The figure of that living Sacrifice;
Who dying, all th'Infernall powres orecame,
That we with him t'Eternitie might rise:
    This pretious Passeover feed upon, O Queene,
    Let your faire Virtues in my Glasse be seene.   90

And she that is the patterne of all Beautie,
The very modell of your Majestie,
Whose rarest parts enforceth Love and Duty,
The perfect patterne of all Pietie:
    O let my Booke by her faire eies be blest,   95
    In whose pure thoughts all Innocency rests.

The Lady Elizabeths Grace.

Then shall I thinke my Glasse a glorious Skie,
When two such glittring Suns at once appeare;
The one repleat with Sov'raigne Majestie,
Both shining brighter than the clearest cleare: 100

Line 85. **Paschal Lambe:** Passover lamb, a figure for Christ, sacrificed for the sins of mankind.

Line 89. **Passeover:** Jewish feast commemorating salvation from the Angel of Death, which passed over houses sprinkled with the blood of a sacrificial lamb but slew the firstborn sons of all others in Egypt (Ex. 12:22–27).

Lines 91–94. **she ... Pietie:** Princess Elizabeth, Anne's daughter.

And both reflecting comfort to my spirits,
To find their grace so much above my merits

Whose untun'd voyce the dolefull notes doth sing
Of sad Affliction in an humble straine;
Much like unto a Bird that wants a wing,   105
And cannot flie, but warbles forth her paine:
  Or he that barred from the Suns bright light,
  Wanting daies comfort, doth comend the night.

So I that live clos'd up in Sorrowes Cell,
Since great *Elizaes* favour blest my youth;   110
And in the confines of all cares doe dwell,
Whose grieved eyes no pleasure ever view'th:
  But in Christs suffrings, such sweet taste they have,
  As makes me praise pale Sorrow and the Grave.

And this great Ladie whom I love and honour,   115
And from my very tender yeeres have knowne,
This holy habite still to take upon her,
Still to remaine *the same*, and still her owne:
  And what our fortunes doe enforce us to,
  She of Devotion and meere Zeale doth do.   120

Which makes me thinke our heavy burden light,
When such a one as she will help to beare it:
Treading the paths that make our way go right,
What garment is so faire but she may weare it;

Line 110. **Elizaes favour**: the good will of Queen Elizabeth I, in whose court Lanyer spent her youth.

Especially for her that entertaines   125
A Glorious Queene, in whome all woorth remains.

Whose powre may raise my sad dejected Muse,
From this lowe Mansion of a troubled mind;
Whose princely favour may such grace infuse,
That I may spread Her Virtues in like kind: 130
    But in this triall of my slender skill,
    I wanted knowledge to performe my will.

For even as they that doe behold the Starres,
Not with the eie of Learning, but of Sight,
To find their motions, want of knowledge barres   135
Although they see them in their brightest light:
    So, though I see the glory of her State,
    Its she that must instruct and elevate.

My weake distempred braine and feeble spirits,
Which all unlearned have adventur'd, this   140
To write of Christ, and of his sacred merits,
Desiring that this Booke Her hands may kisse:
    And though I be unworthy of that grace,
    Yet let her blessed thoghts this book imbrace.

And pardon me (faire Queene) though I presume,   145
To doe that which so many better can;
Not that I Learning to my selfe assume,
Or that I would compare with any man:

Line 126. **Glorious Queene**: Queen Anne.   Line 132. **wanted**: lacked.

But as they are Scholers, and by Art do write,
So Nature yeelds my Soule a sad delight.   150

And since all Arts at first from Nature came,
That goodly Creature, Mother of Perfection,
Whom *Joves* almighty hand at first did frame,
Taking both her and hers in his protection:
    Why should not She now grace my barren Muse,   155
    And in a Woman all defects excuse.

So peerelesse Princesse humbly I desire,
That your great wisedome would vouchsafe t'omit
All faults; and pardon if my spirits retire,
Leaving to ayme at what they cannot hit: 160
    To write your worth, which no pen can expresse,
    Were but t'ecclipse your Fame, and make it lesse.

Line 150. **sad:** solemn, serious.

Line 153. **Joves ... hand:** God as creator of Nature.

Line 154. **her ... hers:** nature and those who claim her influence.

Lines 158–59. **t'omit ... faults:** overlook inadequacies in the verse and presumption in a commoner (Lanyer) addressing a Queen.

Line 162. **t'ecclipse ... Fame:** poetry of praise should promote fame, but its inadequacy in this case would obscure rather than promote it.

To the Lady *Elizabeths* Grace

Most gratious Ladie, faire ELIZABETH,
Whose Name and Virtues puts us still in mind,
Of her, of whom we are depriv'd by death;
The *Phœnix* of her age, whose worth did bind
All worthy minds so long as they have breath,   5
   In linkes of Admiration, love and zeale,
   To that deare Mother of our Common-weale.

Even you faire Princesse next our famous Queene,
I doe invite unto this wholesome feast,
Whose goodly wisedome, though your yeares be greene,   10
By such good workes may daily be increast,
Though your faire eyes farre better Bookes have seene;
   Yet being the first fruits of a womans wit,
   Vouchsafe you favour in accepting it.

Title. **Lady … Grace:** Princess Elizabeth (1596–1662), eldest daughter of King James I and Queen Anne. The dedication to her "grace" is a conventional appeal to her good favor.

Line 3. **her:** the late Queen Elizabeth I, predecessor of King James I.

Line 4. **Phoenix:** mythical bird of great beauty which builds its own funeral pyre and rises again from its own ashes. A symbol of continuity past death and resurrection, often used as a symbol of Queen Elizabeth I.

Line 7. **Common-weale:** commonwealth, state.

Line 9. **wholesome feast:** Lanyer's story of Christ's passion.

Line 13. **first fruits:** the poem, Lanyer's first published effort; an allusion to Christ as the "first fruits of them that slept"—as the first immortal man (I Cor. 15:20).

11

To all vertuous Ladies in generall

Each blessed Lady that in Virtue spends
Your pretious time to beautifie your soules;
Come wait on hir whom winged Fame attends
And in her hand the Booke where she inroules
Those high deserts that Majestie commends: 5
    Let this faire Queene not unattended bee,
    When in my Glasse she daines her selfe to see.

Put on your wedding garments every one,
The Bridegroome stayes to entertaine you all;
Let Virtue be your guide, for she alone   10
Can leade you right that you can never fall;
And make no stay for feare he should be gone:
    But fill your Lamps with oyle of burning zeale,
    That to your Faith he may his Truth reveale.

The roabes that Christ wore before his death.

Let all your roabes be purple scarlet white,   15
Those perfit colours purest Virtue wore,
Come deckt with Lillies that did so delight
To be preferr'd in Beauty, farre before

Line 3. **hir**: Virtue.   Line 5. **deserts**: deservings.

Line 7. **daines**: deigns, sees fit.

Line 9. **Bridegroome**: Christ, God (Isa. 62:5, Mat. 25:1–13).

Line 13. **fill … zeale**: as the wise virgins did for the bridegroom (Mat. 25:1–13).

Lines 17–21. **Come … field**: requests the "vertuous Ladies" to dress in colors that celebrate Christ's passion (Mat. 6:28–29, Luke 12:27).

Wise *Salomon* in all his glory dight:
> Whose royall roabes did no such pleasure yield,   20
> As did the beauteous Lilly of the field.

Adorne your temples with faire *Daphnes* crowne   *In token of*
The never changing Laurel, alwaies greene;   *Constancie.*
Let constant hope all worldly pleasures drowne,
In wise *Minerva's* paths be alwaies seene;   25
Or with bright *Cynthia,* thogh faire *Venus* frown:
> With *Esop* crosse the posts of every doore,
> Where Sinne would riot, making Virtue poore.

And let the Muses your companions be,
Those sacred sisters that on *Pallas* wait;   30
Whose Virtues with the purest minds agree,
Whose godly labours doe avoyd the baite
Of worldly pleasures, living alwaies free
> From sword, from violence, and from ill report,
> To these nine Worthies all faire mindes resort.   35

Line 19. **Salomon:** Solomon, King of ancient Israel known for his splendor and wisdom.   **dight:** dressed.

Line 21. **Lilly:** Mat. 6:28–29.

Line 22. **Daphnes crowne:** in Greek mythology, Daphne was a nymph who was turned into a laurel tree after praying for rescue from Apollo, who was pursuing her.

Line 25. **Minerva:** Roman name for goddess of wisdom.

Line 26. **Cynthia:** goddess of the moon and of chastity.   **Venus:** goddess of beauty and of love.

Line 27. **Esop:** Aesop (c. 6th century B.C.), Greek author of fables.

Line 29. **Muses:** in Greek mythology, nine sisters who inspire and represent the arts.

Line 30. **Pallas:** Pallas Athena, Greek name for the goddess of wisdom; a favorite allegorical self-representation of Queen Anne (in masques, for example).

Annoynt your haire with *Aarons* pretious oyle,
And bring your palmes of vict'ry in your hands,
To overcome all thoughts that would defile
The earthly circuit of your soules faire lands;
Let no dimme shadowes your cleare eyes beguile: 40
    Sweet odours, mirrhe, gum, aloes, frankincense,
    Present that King who di'd for your offence.

Behold, bright *Titans* shining chariot staies,
All deckt with flowers of the freshest hew,
Attended on by Age, Houres, Nights, and Daies,   45
Which alters not your beauty, but gives you
Much more, and crownes you with eternall praise:
    This golden chariot wherein you must ride,
    Let simple Doves, and subtill serpents guide.

Come swifter than the motion of the Sunne,   50
To be transfigur'd with our loving Lord,
Lest Glory end what Grace in you begun,
Of heav'nly riches make your greatest hoord,
In Christ all honour, wealth, and beautie's wonne:
    By whose perfections you appeare more faire   55
    Than *Phoebus*, if he seav'n times brighter were.

Line 36. **Aarons ... oyle:** Moses anointed his brother Aaron with oil to sanctify him as the first priest of Israel (Lev. 8:12).

Line 41. **mirrhe ... frankincense:** used to anoint the dead and to honour a divinity.

Line 43. **Titan:** here, a reference to the god of the sun. Titans were pre-Olympian gods.

Line 45. **Age ... Daies:** in Greek mythology, personified representations of pre-Olympian forces which created and represent time.

Line 49. **simple:** innocent.   **subtill:** clever.

Line 52. **Lest ... begun:** do not let reluctance to accept Christ's death and resurrection cancel the original favor (grace) that God has given you.

Line 53. **hoord:** hoard.   Line 56. **Phoebus:** god of the sun.

Gods holy Angels will direct your Doves,
And bring your Serpents to the fields of rest,
Where he doth stay that purchast all your loves
In bloody torments, when he di'd opprest,   60
There shall you find him in those pleasant groves
   Of sweet *Elizium*, by the Well of Life,
    Whose cristal springs do purge from worldly strife.

Thus may you flie from dull and sensuall earth,
Whereof at first your bodies formed were,   65
That new regen'rate in a second berth,
Your blessed soules may live without all feare,
Beeing immortall, subject to no death:
   But in the eie of heaven so highly placed,
    That others by your virtues may be graced.   70

Where worthy Ladies I will leave you all,
Desiring you to grace this little Booke;
Yet some of you me thinkes I heare to call
Me by my name, and bid me better looke,
Lest unawares I in an error fall: 75
   In generall tearmes, to place you with the rest,
    Whom Fame commends to be the very best.

Line 59. **he**: Christ.

Line 62. **Elizium**: Elysian fields; in Greek mythology, a place of perfect happiness for the blessed after death.

Line 64. **sensuall**: physical.

Line 66. **second berth**: Jesus preached that for salvation a person must be "born again … of water and the spirit" (John 3:3–5).

Lines 76–84. **generall … quake**: Lanyer acknowledges that many of the "vertuous Ladies" she addresses deserve more specific praise, but time and humility allow her only to praise them in general.

Tis true, I must confesse (O noble Fame)
There are a number honoured by thee,
Of which, some few thou didst recite by name,   80
And willd my Muse they should remembred bee;
Wishing some would their glorious Trophies frame:
    Which if I should presume to undertake,
    My tired Hand for very feare would quake.

Onely by name I will bid some of those,   85
That in true Honors seate have long bin placed,
Yea even such as thou hast chiefly chose,
By whom my Muse may be the better graced;
Therefore, unwilling longer time to lose,
    I will invite some Ladies that I know,   90
    But chiefly those as thou hast graced so.

To the Ladie *Arabella*

Great learned Ladie, whom I long have knowne,
And yet not knowne so much as I desired:
Rare *Phoenix*, whose faire feathers are your owne,
With which you flie, and are so much admired:
True honour whom true Fame hath so attired,   5
   In glittering raiment shining much more bright,
   Than silver Starres in the most frostie night.

Come like the morning Sunne new out of bed,
And cast your eyes upon this little Booke,
Although you be so well accompan'ed   10
With *Pallas*, and the Muses, spare one looke
Upon this humbled King, who all forsooke,
   That in his dying armes he might imbrace
   Your beauteous Soule, and fill it with his grace.

Title. **To ... Arabella**: Arbella Stuart (1575–1615), first cousin of James I, had a strong claim to the throne. She was known for her learning, and managed to remain in James's favor until her secret marriage in 1610 to William Seymour, who also had royal blood. James considered the marriage a threat to his own kingship. Lanyer, like many of our contemporaries, used the Latinate spelling of Stuart's name. Stuart herself, however, always signed her name "Arbella."

Line 3. **Phoenix**: mythical bird of great beauty which is reborn from its own ashes.

Line 11. **Pallas**: Athena, Greek goddess of wisdom.   **Muses**: in Greek myth, nine sisters who inspire and represent the arts.

Line 12. **humbled King**: Jesus as presented in Lanyer's "Salve Deus."

To the Ladie *Susan*,
Countesse Dowager of Kent,
and Daughter to the Duchesse of Suffolke

Come you that were the Mistris of my youth,
The noble guide of my ungovern'd dayes;
Come you that have delighted in Gods truth,
Help now your handmaid to sound foorth his praise:
   You that are pleas'd in his pure excellencie,   5
   Vouchsafe to grace this holy feast, and me.

And as your rare Perfections shew'd the Glasse
Wherein I saw each wrinckle of a fault;
You the Sunnes virtue, I that faire greene grasse,
That flourisht fresh by your cleere virtues taught: 10
   For you possest those gifts that grace the mind,
   Restraining youth whom Errour oft doth blind.

In you these noble Virtues did I note,
First, love and feare of God, of Prince, of Lawes,
Rare Patience with a mind so farre remote   15
From worldly pleasures, free from giving cause
   Of least suspect to the most envious eie,
   That in faire Virtues Storehouse sought to prie.

Title. **Ladie Susan**: Susan Bertie, the widow of Reynold Grey of West, Earl of Kent (d. 1573), married Sir John Wingfield in 1581.

Line 6. **holy feast**: the passion of Christ, described in the "Salve Deus" poem.

Line 7. **Glasse**: mirror.

18

Whose Faith did undertake in Infancie,
All dang'rous travells by devouring Seas   20
To flie to Christ from vaine Idolatry,
Not seeking there this worthlesse world to please,
    By your most famous Mother so directed,
    That noble Dutchesse, who liv'd unsubjected.

From *Romes* ridiculous prier and tyranny,   25
That mighty Monarchs kept in awfull feare;
Leaving here her lands, her state, dignitie;
Nay more, vouchsaft disguised weedes to weare:
    When with Christ Jesus she did meane to goe,
    From sweet delights to taste part of his woe.   30

Come you that ever since hath followed her,
In these sweet paths of faire Humilitie;
Contemning Pride pure Virtue to preferre,
Not yeelding to base Imbecillitie,
    Nor to those weake inticements of the world,   35
    That have so many thousand Soules insnarld.

Receive your Love whom you have sought so farre,
Which heere presents himselfe within your view;
Behold this bright and all directing Starre,
Light of your Soule that doth all grace renew: 40

Lines 23–24. **Mother ... Dutchesse**: Catherine Willoughby, Duchess of Suffolk, a renowned Reformation figure of the mid-sixteenth century. During the Catholic Queen Mary's rule of 1553–58 she fled England, taking her infant daughter Susan with her (see lines 19–21).

Line 25. **Romes ... tyranny**: the pope ("prier" or prior) and the papacy.

Line 28. **weedes**: clothes.   Line 37. **your Love**: Christ.

And in his humble paths since you do tread,
Take this faire Bridegroome in your soules pure bed.

And since no former gaine hath made me write,
Nor my desertlesse service could have wonne,
Onely your noble Virtues do incite   45
My Pen, they are the ground I write upon;
    Nor any future profit is expected,
    Then how can these poore lines goe unrespected?

Lines 43–47. **former gaine … future profit**: Lanyer claims to have received no monetary patronage from the Countess Dowager, nor to be asking for any.

Line 44. **desertlesse**: undeserving.

The Authors Dreame to the Ladie *Marie*, the Countesse Dowager of *Pembrooke*

Me thought I pass'd through th' *Edalyan* Groves,
And askt the Graces, if they could direct
Me to a Lady whom *Minerva* chose,
To live with her in height of all respect.

Yet looking backe into my thoughts againe,   5
The eie of Reason did behold her there
Fast ti'd unto them in a golden Chaine,
They stood, but she was set in Honors chaire.

Title. **Ladie Marie:** Mary Sidney, Countess of Pembroke (1561–1621), was the principal female literary figure of her era and a major cultural influence. She was the daughter of Sir Henry Sidney and Mary Dudley (sister of Queen Elizabeth's favorite, Robert, Earl of Leicester); the sister of Sir Philip Sidney; the wife of the Earl of Pembroke; the mother of William Herbert, Earl of Pembroke, and of Philip Herbert, Earl of Montgomery (and of Pembroke and Montgomery after his brother's death). She was also the aunt of Lady Mary Wroth, author of the 1621 pastoral romance, *The Countess of Montgomerie's Urania*. The Countess was the foremost patron of the age, the audience and editor for Sir Philip Sidney's *Arcadia*, and well-known for her poems based on the Psalms (of 150 psalms, Sir Philip wrote versions of 43 before his death in 1586, and the Countess wrote the remaining 107; all 150 were widely circulated in manuscript during the early seventeenth century).

Line 1. **Edalyan:** probably from Idalia, a mountain city in Cyprus, sacred to Venus; possibly from Mt. Ida, home of the muses.

Line 2. **Graces:** in Greek myth, three sisters who bestowed beauty and charm.

Line 3. **Minerva:** Roman name for Athena, Greek goddess of wisdom.

Line 7. **ti'd ... Chaine:** reference to a Platonic theory of the bonds of love.

21

And nine faire Virgins sate upon the ground,
With Harps and Vialls in their lilly hands;   10
Whose harmony had all my sences drown'd,
But that before mine eyes an object stands,

Whose Beauty shin'd like *Titons* cleerest raies,
She blew a brasen Trumpet, which did sound
Throgh al the world that worthy Ladies praise,   15
And by Eternall Fame I saw her crown'd.

The God   Yet studying, if I were awake, or no,
of Dreames. God *Morphy* came and tooke me by the hand,
And wil'd me not from Slumbers bowre to go,
Till I the summe of all did understand.   20

When presently the Welkin that before
Look'd bright and cleere, me thought, was overcast,
And duskie clouds, with boyst'rous winds great store,
Foretold of violent stormes which could not last.

And gazing up into the troubled skie,   25
Me thought a Chariot did from thence descend,
Where one did sit repleat with Majestie,
Drawne by foure fierie Dragons, which did bend

Line 9. **nine ... Virgins**: the muses, who represented and bestowed skill in arts and learning.

Line 10. **Vialls**: viols (early relative of the cello).

Line 14. **brasen**: brass.   Line 18. **Morphy**: Morpheus. See side note.

Line 19. **bowre**: private chamber or inner room.

Line 21. **Welkin**: sky.   Line 27. **repleat**: full.

Their course where this most noble Lady sate,
Whom all these virgins with due reverence   30
Did entertaine, according to that state
Which did belong unto her Excellence.

When bright *Bellona*, so they did her call,   *Goddesse*
Whom these faire Nymphs so humbly did receive,   *of Warre*
                                                                                        and
A manly mayd which was both faire and tall,   35   *Wisdome.*
Her borrowed Charret by a spring did leave.

With speare, and shield, and currat on her breast,
And on her head a helmet wondrous bright,
With myrtle bayes, and olive branches drest,
Wherein me thought I tooke no small delight.   40

To see how all the Graces sought grace here,
And in what meeke, yet princely sort shee came;
How this most noble Lady did imbrace her,
And all humors unto hers did frame.

Now faire *Dictina* by the breake of Day,   45   *The*
With all her Damsels round about her came,   *Moone.*
Ranging the woods to hunt, yet made a stay,
When harkning to the pleasing sound of Fame;

Her Ivory bowe and silver shaftes shee gave
Unto the fairest nymphe of all her traine;   50
And wondring who it was that in so grave,
Yet gallant fashion did her beauty staine:

Line 36. **Charret**: chariot.   Line 37. **currat**: armor.
Line 39. **myrtle … branches**: symbols of victory.

Shee deckt her selfe with all the borrowed light
That *Phoebus* would afford from his faire face,
And made her Virgins to appeare so bright,   55
That all the hils and vales received grace.

Then pressing where this beauteous troupe did stand,
They all received her most willingly,
And unto her the Lady gave her hand,
That shee should keepe with them continually.   60

The
Morning.

Aurora rising from her rosie bedde,
First blusht, then wept, to see faire *Phoebe* grac'd,
And unto Lady *Maie* these wordes shee sed,
Come, let us goe, we will not be out-fac'd.

I will unto *Apolloes* Waggoner,   65
A bidde him bring his Master presently,
That his bright beames may all her Beauty marre,
Gracing us with the luster of his eie.

Come, come, sweet Maie, and fill their laps
      with floures,
And I will give a greater light than she: 70
So all these Ladies favours shall be ours,
None shall be more esteem'd than we shall be.

Line 54. **Phoebus**: the sun; also Apollo.

Line 62. **Phoebe**: like Dictina, a name for the goddess of the moon; also Cynthia, Diana.

Line 63. **Lady Maie**: goddess of spring and flowers; also Flora.

Thus did *Aurora* dimme faire *Phœbus* light,
And was receiv'd in bright *Cynthiaes* place,
While *Flora* all with fragrant floures dight,   75
Pressed to shew the beauty of her face.

Though these, me thought, were verie pleasing sights,
Yet now these Worthies did agree to go,
Unto a place full of all rare delights,
A place that yet *Minerva* did not know.   80

That sacred Spring where Art and Nature striv'd
Which should remaine as Sov'raigne of the place;
Whose antient quarrell being new reviv'd,
Added fresh Beauty, gave farre greater Grace.

To which as umpiers now these Ladies go,   85
Judging with pleasure their delightfull case;
Whose ravisht sences made them quickely know,
T'would be offensive either to displace.

And therefore will'd they should for ever dwell,
In perfit unity by this matchlesse Spring: 90
Since 'twas impossible either should excell,
Or her faire fellow in subjection bring.

But here in equall sov'raigntie to live,
Equall in state, equall in dignitie,
That unto others they might comfort give,   95
Rejoycing all with their sweet unitie.

Line 73. **Aurora**: goddess of the dawn, or morning.   Line 75. **dight**: dressed.
Line 85. **umpiers**: umpires; arbitrators.

And now me thought I long to heare her name,
Whom wise *Minerva* honoured so much,
Shee whom I saw was crownd by noble Fame,
Whom Envy sought to sting, yet could not tuch.   100

Me thought the meager elfe did seeke bie waies
To come unto her, but it would not be;
Her venime purifi'd by virtues raies,
Shee pin'd and starv'd like an Anotomie:

While beauteous *Pallas* with this Lady faire,   105
Attended by these Nymphs of noble fame,
Beheld those woods, those groves, those bowers rare,
By which *Pergusa*, for so hight the name

Of that faire spring, his dwelling place & ground;
And throgh those fields with sundry flowers clad,   110
Of sev'rall colours, to adorne the ground,
And please the sences ev'n of the most sad:

He trayld along the woods in wanton wise,
With sweet delight to entertaine them all;
Inviting them to sit and to devise   115
On holy hymnes; at last to mind they call

Line 104. **Anotomie:** emaciated body.   Line 105. **Pallas:** Athena, Minerva.
Line 108. **hight:** was named.   Line 110. **sundry:** various.
Line 112. **sad:** serious minded.   Line 113. **wanton wise:** playful manner.

Those rare sweet songs which *Israels* King did frame
Unto the Father of Eternitie;
Before his holy wisedom tooke the name
Of great *Messias*, Lord of unitie.

Those holy Sonnets they did all agree,
With this most lovely Lady here to sing;
That by her noble breasts sweet harmony,
Their musicke might in eares of Angels ring.

While saints like Swans about this silver brook
Should *Hallalu-iah* sing continually,
Writing her praises in th'eternall booke
Of endlesse honour, true fames memorie.

Thus I in sleep the heavenli'st musicke hard,
That ever earthly eares did entertaine;
And durst not wake, for feare to be debard
Of what my sences sought still to retaine.

Yet sleeping, praid dull Slumber to unfold
Her noble name, who was of all admired;
When presently in drowsie tearmes he told
Not onely that, but more than I desired.

The Psalms written newly by the Countesse Dowager of Penbrooke.

120

125

130

135

Line 117. **Israels King:** David, the psalmist.
Side note. **Penbrooke:** alternative Renaissance spelling for Pembroke.
Line 129. **hard:** heard.

This nymph, quoth he, great *Penbrooke* hight by name,
Sister to valiant *Sidney,* whose cleere light
Gives light to all that tread true paths of Fame,
Who in the globe of heav'n doth shine so bright;   140

That beeing dead, his fame doth him survive,
Still living in the hearts of worthy men;
Pale Death is dead, but he remaines alive,
Whose dying wounds restor'd him life agen.

And this faire earthly goddesse which you see,   145
Bellona and her virgins doe attend;
In virtuous studies of Divinitie,
Her pretious time continually doth spend.

So that a Sister well shee may be deemd,
To him that liv'd and di'd so nobly;   150
And farre before him is to be esteemd
For virtue, wisedome, learning, dignity.

Whose beauteous soule hath gain'd a double life,
Both here on earth, and in the heav'ns above,
Till dissolution end all worldly strife: 155
Her blessed spirit remaines, of holy love,

Directing all by her immortall light,
In this huge sea of sorrowes, griefes, and feares;

Line 138. **Sidney**: Lady Mary's brother, Sir Philip Sidney (1554–86).

Lines 143–44. **he … agen**: Sidney died in an attack on a Spanish convoy in the Netherlands and instantly became a legendary model for the heroic poet.

Line 146. **Bellona**: goddess of war and wisdom; see Lanyer's side note to line 33.

With contemplation of Gods powrefull might,
Shee fils the eies, the hearts, the tongues, the eares   160

Of after-comming ages, which shall reade
Her love, her zeale, her faith, and pietie;
The faire impression of whose worthy deed,
Seales her pure soule unto the Deitie.

That both in Heav'n and Earth it may remaine,   165
Crownd with her Makers glory and his love;
And this did Father Slumber tell with paine,
Whose dulnesse scarce could suffer him to move.

When I awaking left him and his bowre,
Much grieved that I could no longer stay;   170
Sencelesse was sleepe, not to admit me powre,
As I had spent the night to spend the day:

Then had God *Morphie* shew'd the end of all,
And what my heart desir'd, mine eies had seene;
For as I wak'd me thought I heard one call   175
For that bright Charet lent by *Joves* faire Queene.

But thou, base cunning thiefe, that robs our sprits
Of halfe that span of life which yeares doth give;
And yet no praise unto thy selfe it merits,   *To Sleepe.*
To make a seeming death in those that live.   180

Lines 171–72. **Sencelesse ... day**: sleep has no power to let her enjoy her dream during the day.

Line 176. **Joves ... Queene**: Juno, queen of the gods.   Line 177. **sprits**: spirits.

Yea wickedly thou doest consent to death,
Within thy restfull bed to rob our soules;
In Slumbers bowre thou steal'st away our breath,
Yet none there is that thy base stealths controules.

If poore and sickly creatures would imbrace thee,   185
Or they to whom thou giv'st a taste of pleasure,
Thou fli'st as if *Acteons* hounds did chase thee,
Or that to stay with them thou hadst no leasure.

But though thou hast depriv'd me of delight,
By stealing from me ere I was aware;   190
I know I shall enjoy the selfe same sight,
Thou hast no powre my waking sprites to barre.

For to this Lady now I will repaire,
Presenting her the fruits of idle houres;
Thogh many Books she writes that are more rare,   195
Yet there is hony in the meanest flowres:

Which is both wholesome, and delights the taste:
Though sugar be more finer, higher priz'd,
Yet is the painefull Bee no whit disgrac'd,
Nor her faire wax, or hony more despiz'd.   200

And though that learned damsell and the rest,
Have in a higher style her Trophie fram'd;

Line 187. **Acteons hounds**: the mythological hunter Acteon was turned into a stag and chased by his own hounds.

Line 195. **rare**: valuable, of exceptional merit.

Line 196. **meanest**: lowest, least appealing.

Line 199. **painefull**: laboring, taking pains.   **no whit**: not at all.

Yet these unlearned lines beeing my best,
Of her great wisedom can no whit be blam'd.

And therefore, first I here present my Dreame,   205
And next, invite her Honour to my feast,
For my cleare reason sees her by that streame,
Where her rare virtues daily are increast.

So craving pardon for this bold attempt,
I here present my mirrour to her view,   210
Whose noble virtues cannot be exempt,
My Glasse beeing steele, declares them to be true.

And Madame, if you will vouchsafe that grace,
To grace those flowres that springs from virtues ground;
Though your faire mind on worthier workes is plac'd,   215
On workes that are more deepe, and more profound;

Yet is it no disparagement to you,
To see your Saviour in a Shepheards weed,
Unworthily presented in your viewe,
Whose worthinesse will grace each line you reade.   220

Receive him here by my unworthy hand,
And reade his paths of faire humility;
Who though our sinnes in number passe the sand,
They all are purg'd by his Divinity.

Line 206. **feast:** Lanyer's poem on Christ's passion.

Line 212. **Glasse ... steele:** the "steel glass" was conventionally a truthful mirror.

Line 218. **Shepheards weed:** shepherd's clothes; Christ was often compared to a good shepherd (John 10:11–17).

To the Ladie *Lucie*, Countesse of Bedford

Me thinkes I see faire Virtue readie stand,
T'unlocke the closet of your lovely breast,
Holding the key of Knowledge in her hand,
Key of that Cabbine where your selfe doth rest,
To let him in, by whom her youth was blest   5
   The true-love of your soule, your hearts delight,
   Fairer than all the world in your cleare sight.

He that descended from celestiall glory,
To taste of our infirmities and sorrowes,
Whose heavenly wisdom read the earthly storie   10
Of fraile Humanity, which his godhead borrows;
Loe here he coms all stucke with pale deaths arrows:
   In whose most pretious wounds your soule may reade
   Salvation, while he (dying Lord) doth bleed.

Title. **Ladie Lucie**: Lucie, Countess of Bedford (d. 1627) was the niece of John Harrington, Elizabethan translator of Ariosto. She married the third Earl of Bedford in 1594 and quickly distinguished herself as a writer and as a friend and patron of writers, including Daniel, Drayton, Jonson, and Donne. After the Countess of Pembroke, she was the most important patron of her day and a frequent dedicatee of Jacobean poets.

Line 2. **closet**: small private room.

Line 4. **Cabbine**: cabinet, or "closet" (as above); here, an allusion to the heart.

Line 5. **him**: Christ.   Line 11. **Humanity ... borrows**: God borrows human form.

Line 12. **stucke ... arrows**: Christ's passion is here figured in a popular image of the martyrdom of St. Sebastian.

You whose cleare Judgement farre exceeds my skil, 15
Vouchsafe to entertaine this dying lover,
The Ocean of true grace, whose streames doe fill
All those with Joy, that can his love recover;
About this blessed Arke bright Angels hover:
    Where your faire soule may sure and safely rest, 20
    When he is sweetly seated in your brest.

There may your thoughts as servants to your heart,
Give true attendance on this lovely guest,
While he doth to that blessed bowre impart
Flowres of fresh comforts, decke that bed of rest, 25
With such rich beauties as may make it blest:
    And you in whom all raritie is found,
    May be with his eternall glory crownd.

Line 16. **entertaine**: receive.

Line 19. **Arke**: as in the Old Testament ark (or holder) of the covenant, a place where God's word resides; here, Lanyer's "Salve Deus" poem, containing the story of the New Testament, or covenant.

Line 27. **raritie**: excellence of character.

To the Ladie *Margaret*
Countesse Dowager of Cumberland

Right Honourable and Excellent Lady, I may say with Saint
*Peter, Silver nor gold have I none, but such as I have, that give
I you:* for having neither rich pearles of India, nor fine gold of
Arabia, nor diamonds of inestimable value; neither those rich
treasures, Arramaticall Gums, incense, and sweet odours, which
were presented by those Kingly Philosophers to the babe Jesus I
present unto you even our Lord Jesus himselfe, whose infinit
value is not to be comprehended within the weake imagination
or wit of man: and as Saint *Peter* gave health to the body, so I
10 deliver you the health of the soule; which is this most pretious
pearle of all perfection, this rich diamond of devotion, this perfect gold growing in the veines of that excellent earth of the
most blessed Paradice, wherein our second *Adam* had his restlesse habitation. The sweet incense, balsums, odours, and
gummes that flowes from that beautifull tree of Life, sprung

Title. **Ladie Margaret**: Margaret, Countess Dowager of Cumberland (d. 1616), was
Lanyer's principal patron and dedicate of the "Salve Deus" poem itself. Born
Margaret Russell, daughter of the second Earl of Bedford, she married George,
third Earl of Cumberland in 1577, and in 1590 produced their only child, Anne (later
Countess of Dorset, or Dorcet. See Introduction, page xxv). For what is known of the
relationships among Margaret, Anne, and Lanyer, see Lewalski, "Re-writing
Patriarchy."

Lines 1–3. **Saint Peter ... you**: Acts 3:2–8.   Line 5. **Arramaticall**: aromatic.

Line 6. **Kingly Philosophers**: wise men, magi.   Line 9. **wit**: intelligence.

Lines 10–11. **this ... pearle**: the story of Christ in the "Salve Deus" poem.

Lines 15–16. **tree ... Jessie**: Christ; Jesus was of the line of David, whose father was
Jesse (Ruth 4:22).

from the roote of *Jessie*,which is so super-excellent, that it giveth
grace to the meanest & most unworthy hand that will undertake to write thereof; neither can it receive any blemish thereby:
for as a right diamond can loose no whit of his beautie by the
blacke foyle underneath it, neither by beeing placed in the   20
darke, but retaines his naturall beauty and brightnesse shining
in greater perfection than before; so this most pretious diamond, for beauty and riches exceeding all the most pretious diamonds and rich jewels of the world can receive no blemish, nor
impeachment, by my unworthy hand writing; but wil with the
Sunne retaine his owne brightnesse and most glorious lustre,
though never so many blind eyes looke upon him. Therefore
good Madame, to the most perfect eyes of your understanding,
I deliver the inestimable treasure of all elected soules, to bee
perused at convenient times; as also, the mirrour of your most   30
worthy minde, which may remaine in the world many yeares
longer than your Honour, or my selfe can live, to be a light unto
those that come after, desiring to tread in the narrow path of virtue, that leads the way to heaven. In which way, I pray God send
your Honour long to continue, that your light may so shine
before men, that they may glorifie your father which is in
Heaven: and that I and many others may follow you in the same
tracke. So wishing you in this world all increase of health and
honour, and in the world to come life everlasting, I rest.

Line 17. **meanest**: simplest, most humble.

Line 20. **foyle**: a thin leaf of some metal placed under a precious stone to increase its
brilliancy; the setting (of a jewel).

Line 25. **impeachment**: damage, injury.

Line 29. **elected**: chosen (by God) to be saved from damnation.

Line 32. **your Honour**: your honorable self.   Line 33. **narrow path**: Mat. 7:14.

Line 35. **your light**: Mat. 5:16.

To the Ladie *Katherine* Countesse of Suffolke

Although great Lady, it may seeme right strange,
That I a stranger should presume thus farre,
To write to you; yet as the times doe change,
So are we subject to that fatall starre,
    Under the which we were produc'd to breath,   5
    That starre that guides us even untill our death.

And guided me to frame this worke of grace,
Not of it selfe, but by celestiall powres,
To which, both that and wee must needs give place,
Since what we have, we cannot count it ours: 10
    For health, wealth, honour, sicknesse, death and all,
    Is in Gods powre, which makes us rise and fall.

And since his powre hath given me powre to write,
A subject fit for you to looke upon,
Wherein your soule may take no small delight,   15
When her bright eyes beholds that holy one:

Title. **Ladie Katherine**: Katherine, daughter of Sir Henry Knevet and widow of Richard, eldest son of Robert, Lord Rich, married in 1583 Lord Admiral Thomas Howard, of an old and powerful family. She had a reputation as a powerful and acquisitive woman, but her interest in learning is suggested by receptions she gave at Magdalene College, Cambridge, when her husband was chancellor of the University (*DNB* 10.72–73).

Line 4. **fatall starre**: astrologically-determined destiny, fate; cf. line 8, **celestiall powres.**

Line 14. **subject**: Christ's passion.

By whose great wisedome, love, and speciall grace,
Shee was created to behold his face.

Vouchsafe sweet Lady, to accept these lines,
Writ by a hand that doth desire to doe   20
All services to you whose worth combines
The worthi'st minds to love and honour you:
    Whose beautie, wisedome, children, high estate,
    Doe all concurre to make you fortunate.

But chiefly your most honorable Lord,   25
Whose noble virtues Fame can ne'r forget:
His hand being alwayes ready to afford
Help to the weake, to the unfortunate:
    All which begets more honour and respect,
    Than *Crœsus* wealth, or *Cæsars* sterne aspect.   30

And rightly sheweth that hee is descended
Of honourable *Howards* antient house,
Whose noble deedes by former times commended,
Do now remaine in your most loyall Spouse,
    On whom God powres all blessings from above,   35
    Wealth, honour, children and a worthy Love;

Which is more deare to him than all the rest,
You being the loving Hinde and pleasant Roe,
Wife of his youth, in whom his soule is blest,

Line 25. **honorable Lord**: her husband, Thomas Howard.

Line 30. **Croessus**: fifth century BC Greek king legendary for his wealth.

Line 38. **Hinde, Roe**: words for deer; in English poetry, a popular pun on "dear."

Fountaine from whence his chiefe delights do flow.   40
    Faire tree from which the fruit of Honor springs,
    Heere I present to you the King of kings:

Desiring you to take a perfit view,
Of those great torments Patience did indure;
And reape those Comforts that belongs to you,   45
Which his most painfull death did then assure:
    Writing the Covenant with his pretious blood,
    That your faire soule might bathe her in that flood.

And let your noble daughters likewise reade
This little Booke that I present to you;   50
On heavenly food let them vouchsafe to feede;
Heere they may see a Lover much more true
    Than ever was since first the world began,
    This poore rich King that di'd both God and man.

Yea, let those Ladies which do represent   55
All beauty, wisedome, zeale, and love,
Receive this jewell from *Jehova* sent,
This spotlesse Lambe, this perfit patient Dove:
    Of whom faire *Gabriel*, Gods bright *Mercury*,
    Brought downe a message from the Deitie.   60

Lines 40–41. **Fountaine ... Honor:** mother of his children.

Line 42. **King of kings:** Christ.

Line 43. **perfit:** perfect.   Line 44. **Patience:** Christ.

Line 47. **Covenant ... blood:** reference to the belief that Christ's sacrifice inaugurated a new covenant, or relationship, between God and humankind.

Line 58. **Lambe ... Dove:** Christ.

Line 59. **Gabriel:** God's messenger who announced the coming of Christ to Mary. **Mercury:** messenger for the classical gods, especially Jove.

Here may they see him in a flood of teares,
Crowned with thornes, and bathing in his blood;
Here may they see his feares exceed all feares,
When Heaven in Justice flat against him stood:
    And loathsome death with grim and gastly look,   65
    Presented him that blacke infernall booke,

Wherein the sinnes of all the world were writ,
In deepe Characters of due punishment;
And naught but dying breath could cancel it:
Shame, death, and hell must make the attonement: 70
    Shewing their evidence, seizing wrongful Right,
    Placing heav'ns Beauty in deaths darkest night.

Yet through the sable Clowdes of Shame & Death,
His beauty shewes more clearer than before;
Death lost his strength when he did loose his breath: 75
As fire supprest doth shine and flame the more,
    So in Deaths ashie pale discoloured face,
    Fresh beauty shin'd, yeelding farre greater grace.

No Dove, no Swan, nor Iv'rie could compare
With this faire corps, when 'twas by death imbrac'd;   80
No rose, nor no vermillion halfe so faire
As was that pretious blood that interlac'd
    His body, which bright Angels did attend,
    Waiting on him that must to Heaven ascend.

Line 70. **attonement:** Christ's death must expiate humanity's sins.
Line 75. **his ...he:** Death's ... Christ.   Line 79. **Iv'rie:** ivory.

In whom is all that Ladies can desire;   85
If Beauty, who hath bin more faire than he?
If Wisedome, doth not all the world admire
The depth of his, that cannot searched be?
    If wealth, if honour, fame, or Kingdoms store,
    Who ever liv'd that was possest of more?   90

If zeale, if grace, if love, if pietie,
If constancie, if faith, if faire obedience,
If valour, patience, or sobrietie;
If chast behaviour, meekenesse, continence,
    If justice, mercie, bountie, charitie,   95
    Who can compare with his Divinitie?

Whose vertues more than thoughts can apprehend,
I leave to their more cleere imagination,
That will vouchsafe their borrowed time to spend
In meditating, and in contemplation   100
    Of his rare parts, true honours faire prospect,
    The perfect line that goodnesse doth direct.

And unto you I wish those sweet desires,
That from your perfect thoughts doe daily spring,
Increasing still pure, bright, and holy fires,   105
Which sparkes of pretious grace, by faith doe spring:
    Mounting your soule unto eternall rest,
    There to live happily among the best.

Line 94. **continence**: self-restraint.

Line 106. **grace ... faith**: the doctrine that faith in Christ results in God's grace, or blessings.

To the Ladie *Anne,* Countesse of Dorcet

To you I dedicate this worke of Grace,
This frame of Glory which I have erected,
For your faire mind I hold the fittest place,
Where virtue should be setled & protected;
If highest thoughts true honor do imbrace,   5
And holy Wisdom is of them respected:
    Then in this Mirrour let your faire eyes looke,
    To view your virtues in this blessed Booke.

Blest by our Saviours merits, not my skil,
Which I acknowledge to be very small;   10
Yet if the least part of his blessed Will
I have perform'd, I count I have done all:
One sparke of grace sufficient is to fill
Our Lampes with oyle, ready when he doth call
    To enter with the Bridegroome to the feast,   15
    Where he that is the greatest may be least.

Title. **Ladie Anne:** Anne Clifford (1590–1676), was the only surviving child of George, Duke of Cumberland (d. 1605). In 1609 she married Richard Sackville, Earl of Dorset; after his death, she married Philip Herbert, Earl of Pembroke and Montgomery (in 1630). With the original assistance of her mother, Margaret Clifford, she was a formidable champion of her right to inherit her father's properties in Yorkshire and Westmoreland (which she finally gained in 1643, and ruled actively from 1649 until her death 27 years later); she was also a diarist and family chronicler. See Lewalski, "Re-writing Patriarchy," 90.

Lines 13–15. **sparke … Bridegroome:** reference to Jesus' parable of readiness to serve God (Mat. 25:1–13).

41

Greatnesse is no sure frame to build upon,
No worldly treasure can assure that place;
God makes both even, the Cottage with the Throne,
All worldly honours there are counted base;   20
Those he holds deare, and reckneth as his owne,
Whose virtuous deeds by his especially grace
   Have gain'd his love, his kingdome, and his crowne,
   Whom in the booke of Life he hath set downe.

Titles of honour which the world bestowes,   25
To none but to the virtuous doth belong;
As beauteous bowres where true worth should repose,
And where his dwellings should be built most strong:
But when they are bestow'd upon her foes,
Poore virtues friends indure the greatest wrong: 30
   For they must suffer all indignity,
   Untill in heav'n they better graced be.

What difference was there when the world began,
Was it not Virtue that distinguisht all?
All sprang but from one woman and one man,   35
Then how doth Gentry come to rise and fall?
Or who is he that very rightly can
Distinguish of his birth, or tell at all,

Line 19. **God ... Throne**: all social classes are equal in the sight of God. The poem's major theme is that virtue is true nobility (lines 20–34), which allows Lanyer to claim a kind of equal footing with Anne (see lines 57–64). This thematic approach, though a pious cliché, is probably also intended as comfort for Anne in her frustrating effort to inherit some of her father's noble titles and estates.

Line 27. **bowres**: bowers, pleasant restful places.

Lines 35–36. **All ... fall**: perhaps an echo allusion to "When Adam delved and Eve span, / Who was then the gentleman?"

In what meane state his Ancestors have bin,
Before some one of worth did honour win?   40

Whose successors, although they beare his name,
Possessing not the riches of his minde,
How doe we know they spring out of the same
True stocke of honour, beeing not of that kind?
It is faire virtue gets immortall fame,   45
Tis that doth all love and duty bind:
    If he that much enjoyes, doth little good,
    We may suppose he comes not of that blood.

Nor is he fit for honour, or command,
If base affections over-rules his mind;   50
Or that selfe-will doth carry such a hand,
As worldly pleasures have the powre to blind
So as he cannot see, nor understand
How to discharge that place to him assign'd:
    Gods Stewards must for all the poore provide,   55
    If in Gods house they purpose to abide.

To you, as to Gods Steward I doe write,
In whom the seeds of virtue have bin sowne,
By your most worthy mother, in whose right,
All her faire parts you challenge as your owne;   60

Line 39. **meane:** low.

Lines 47–48. **If ... blood:** an unvirtuous heir of virtuous ancestry might actually be a bastard (though the context allows for a figurative bastardy as well).

Line 54. **discharge ... place:** accomplish the duties of his position.

Line 55. **Stewards:** officials who manage estates for their masters.

Line 56. **purpose:** intend.

If you, sweet Lady, will appeare as bright
As ever creature did that time hath knowne,
   Then weare this Diadem I present to thee,
   Which I have fram'd for her Eternitie.

You are the Heire apparant of this Crowne   65
Of goodnesse, bountie, grace, love, pietie,
By birth its yours, then keepe it as your owne,
Defend it from all base indignitie;
The right your Mother hath to it, is knowne
Best unto you, who reapt such fruit thereby: 70
   This Monument of her faire worth retaine
   In your pure mind, and keepe it from al staine.

And as your Ancestors at first possest
Their honours, for their honourable deeds,
Let their faire virtues never be transgrest,   75
Bind up the broken, stop the wounds that bleeds,
Succour the poore, comfort the comfortlesse,
Cherish faire plants, suppresse unwholsom weeds;
   Although base pelfe do chance to come in place,
   Yet let true worth receive your greatest grace.   80

So shal you shew from whence you are descended,
And leave to all posterities your fame,
So will your virtues alwaies be commended,
And every one will reverence your name;

Line 63. **Diadem**: crown.   Line 77. **Succour**: help.
Line 79. **pelfe**: riches.   Line 82. **posterities**: descendants.

So this poore worke of mine shalbe defended 85
From any scandall that the world can frame:
    And you a glorious Actor will appeare
    Lovely to all, but unto God most deare.

I know right well these are but needlesse lines,
To you, that are so perfect in your part, 90
Whose birth and education both combines;
Nay more than both, a pure and godly heart,
So well instructed to such faire designes,
By your deere Mother, that there needs no art:
    Your ripe discretion in your tender yeares, 95
    By all your actions to the world appeares.

I doe but set a candle in the sunne,
And adde one drop of water to the sea,
Virtue and Beautie both together run,
When you were borne, within your breast to stay; 100
Their quarrell ceast, which long before begun,
They live in peace, and all doe them obey:
    In you faire Madame, are they richly plac'd,
    Where all their worth by Eternity is grac'd.

You goddesse-like unto the world appeare, 105
Inricht with more than fortune can bestowe,
Goodnesse and Grace, which you doe hold more deere
Than worldly wealth, which melts away like snowe;
Your pleasure is the word of God to heare,
That his most holy precepts you may know: 110
    Your greatest honour, faire and virtuous deeds,
    Which from the love and feare of God proceeds.

Therefore to you (good Madame) I present
His lovely love, more worth than purest gold,
Who for your sake his pretious blood hath spent,   115
His death and passion here you may behold,
And view this Lambe, that to the world was sent,
Whom your faire soule may in her armes infold:
    Loving his love, that did endure such paine,
    That you in heaven a worthy place might gaine.   120

For well you knowe, this world is but a Stage
Where all doe play their parts, and must be gone;
Here's no respect of persons, youth, nor age,
Death seizeth all, he never spareth one,
None can prevent or stay that tyrants rage,   125
But Jesus Christ the Just: By him alone
    He was orecome, He open set the dore
    To Eternall life, ne're seene, nor knowne before.

He is the stone the builders did refuse,
Which you, sweet Lady, are to build upon;   130
He is the rocke that holy Church did chuse,
Among which number, you must needs be one;
Faire Shepheardesse, tis you that he will use
To feed his flocke, that trust in him alone:
    All worldly blessings he vouchsafes to you,   135
    That to the poore you may returne his due.

Line 114. **His ... love**: Christ's passion as portrayed in Lanyer's poem.

Line 117. **Lambe**: Christ.

Lines 121–22. **world ... parts**: an Elizabethan commonplace, most familiar from Shakespeare's *As You Like It* (II.vii.139–40); see also Spenser's *Amoretti* 54.

Lines 133–34. **Shepheardesse ... flocke**: Lanyer sees apostolic power in Anne (John 21: 15–17).

And if deserts a Ladies love may gaine,
Then tell me, who hath more deserv'd than he?
Therefore in recompence of all his paine,
Bestowe your paines to reade, and pardon me,   140
If out of wants, or weakenesse of my braine,
I have not done this worke sufficiently;
    Yet lodge him in the closet of your heart,
    Whose worth is more than can be shew'd by Art.

Line 137. **deserts**: deservings.

To the Vertuous Reader

Often have I heard, that it is the property of some women, not only to emulate the virtues and perfections of the rest, but also by all their powers of ill speaking, to ecclipse the brightnes of their deserved fame: now contrary to this custome, which men I hope unjustly lay to their charge, I have written this small volume, or little booke, for the generall use of all virtuous Ladies and Gentlewomen of this kingdome; and in commendation of some particular persons of our owne sexe, such as for the most part, are so well knowne to my selfe, and others, that I dare undertake Fame dares not to call any better. And this have I done, to make knowne to the world, that all women deserve not to be blamed though some forgetting they are women themselves, and in danger to be condemned by the words of their owne mouthes, fall into so great an errour, as to speake unadvisedly against the rest of their sexe; which if it be true, I am perswaded they can shew their owne imperfection in nothing more: and therefore could wish (for their owne ease, modesties, and credit) they would referre such points of folly, to be practised by evill disposed men, who forgetting they were borne of women, nourished of women, and that if it were not by the means of women, they would be quite extinguished out of the world, and a finall ende of them all, doe like Vipers deface the wombes wherein they were bred, onely to give way and utterance to their want of discretion and goodnesse. Such as these, were they that dishonoured Christ his Apostles and Prophets,

---

Line 2. **emulate**: rival, seek to overcome.

putting them to shamefull deaths. Therefore we are not to regard any imputations, that they undeservedly lay upon us, no otherwise than to make use of them to our owne benefits, as spurres to vertue, making us flie all occasions that may colour their unjust speeches to passe currant. Especially considering 30 that they have tempted even the patience of God himselfe, who gave power to wise and virtuous women, to bring downe their pride and arrogancie. As was cruell *Cesarus* by the discreet counsell of noble *Deborah*, Judge and Prophetesse of Israel: and resolution of *Jael* wife of *Heber* the Kenite: wicked *Haman*, by the divine prayers and prudent proceedings of beautifull *Hester:* blasphemous *Holofernes*, by the invincible courage, rare wisdome, and confident carriage of *Judeth:* & the unjust Judges, by the innocency of chast *Susanna:* with infinite others, which for brevitie sake I will omit. As also in respect it pleased our Lord 40 and Saviour Jesus Christ, without the assistance of man, beeing free from originall and all other sinnes, from the time of his conception, till the houre of his death, to be begotten of a woman, borne of a woman, nourished of a woman, obedient to a woman; and that he healed woman, pardoned women, comforted women: yea, even when he was in his greatest agonie and

---

Lines 29–30. **occasions ... currant:** that would offer examples that would make their charges against women seem authentic. **passe currant:** be useable as authentic currency.

Lines 33–34. **Cesarus ... Deborah:** Judg. 4:10–17 ("Cesarus," Sisera). Deborah urged Barak to attack their enemy Sisera.

Line 35. **Jael ... Heber:** Judg. 4:18–22. Sisera took refuge in the house of Jael, wife of Heber; she killed him by hammering a tent peg through his skull.

Lines 35–36. **Haman ... Hester:** Esth. 5–7. Queen Esther interceded on behalf of her people the Jews and had their enemy Haman hanged.

Lines 37–38. **Holofernes ... Judeth:** from the Apocryphal Book of Judith 8–13; she saved her town from Nebuchadnezzar's army by decapitating his general, Holofernes.

Lines 38–39. **Judges ... Susanna:** from the Apocryphal History of Daniel and Susanna; she was falsely accused of unchastity by two men whose advances she had rejected, but the prophet Daniel uncovered their lies and they were put to death.

bloodie sweat, going to be crucified, and also in the last houre
of his death, tooke care to dispose of a woman: after his resurrection, appeared first to a woman, sent a woman to declare his
50 most glorious resurrection to the rest of his Disciples. Many
other examples I could alleadge of divers faithfull and virtuous
women, who have in all ages, not onely beene Confessors, but
also indured most cruel martyrdome for their faith in Jesus
Christ. All which is sufficient to inforce all good Christians and
honourable minded men to speake reverently of our sexe, and
especially of all virtuous and good women. To the modest sen-
sures of both which, I refer these my imperfect indeavours,
knowing that according to their owne excellent dispositions,
they will rather, cherish, nourish, and increase the least sparke
60 of virtue where they find it, by their favourable and best inter-
pretations, than quench it by wrong constructions. To whom I
wish all increase of virtue, and desire their best opinions.

Line 48. **dispose ... woman:** from the cross, Jesus directed a disciple (traditionally,
John) to take care of his mother (John 19:25–27).

Line 49. **appeared ... woman:** Jesus in his resurrection appeared first to Mary
Magdalene and "the other Mary," and sent them to tell the other disciples (Mat.
28:8–10).

Salve Deus Rex Judæorum

Sith *Cynthia* is ascended to that rest
Of endlesse joy and true Eternitie,
That glorious place that cannot be exprest
By any wight clad in mortalitie,
In her almightie love so highly blest,   5
And crown'd with everlasting Sov'raigntie;
    Where Saints and Angells do attend her Throne,
    And she gives glorie unto God alone.

To thee great Countesse now I will applie   *The Ladie*
My Pen, to write thy never dying fame;   10   *Margaret*
That when to Heav'n thy blessed Soule shall flie,   *Countesse*
These lines on earth record thy reverend name: *Dowager of*
And to this taske I meane my Muse to tie,   *Cumberland.*
Though wanting skill I shall but purchase blame:
    Pardon (deere Ladie) want of womans wit   15
    To pen thy praise, when few can equall it.

And pardon (Madame) though I do not write
Those praisefull lines of that delightful place,

Line 1. **Cynthia**: Queen Elizabeth I, figured as the goddess of the moon.

Line 4. **wight**: person.

Line 13. **Muse**: mythical figure who inspires and grants skill in arts and learning.

Lines 17–18. **write ... place**: possibly a reference to a real or feigned request from the Dowager Countess of Cumberland that Lanyer write a description of the beauty of Cooke-ham, the country house that is the topic of this volume's concluding poem.

51

As you commaunded me in that faire night,
When shining *Phoebe* gave so great a grace,   20
Presenting *Paradice* to your sweet sight,
Unfolding all the beauty of her face
    With pleasant groves, hills, walks and stately trees,
    Which pleasures with retired minds agrees.

Whose Eagles eyes behold the glorious Sunne   25
Of th'all-creating Providence, reflecting
His blessed beames on all by him, begunne;
Increasing, strengthning, guiding and directing
All wordly creatures their due course to runne,
Unto His powrefull pleasure all subjecting: 30
    And thou (deere Ladie) by his speciall grace,
    In these his creatures dost behold his face.

Whose all-reviving beautie, yeelds such joyes
To thy sad Soule, plunged in waves of woe,
That worldly pleasures seemes to thee as toyes,   35
Onely thou seek'st Eternitie to know,
Respecting not the infinite annoyes
That Satan to thy well-staid mind can show;
    Ne can he quench in thee, the Spirit of Grace,
    Nor draw thee from beholding Heavens bright face.   40

Line 20. **Phoebe**: the moon; Cynthia, Diana.

Line 37. **infinite annoyes**: generally, Satan's continual attacks on the godly soul; specifically, the trouble Margaret continued to have from relatives, judges, and courtiers as she sought to secure her daughter Anne's inheritance from Margaret's late husband. See title note to the poem on Anne, Countess of Dorset, 41.

Line 38. **well-staid**: well supported, firm.

Thy Mind so perfect by thy Maker fram'd
No vaine delights can harbour in thy heart,
With his sweet love, thou art so much inflam'd,
As of the world thou seem'st to have no part;
So, love him still, thou need'st not be asham'd,   45
Tis He that made thee, what thou wert, and art:
   Tis He that dries all teares from Orphans eies,
   And heares from heav'n the wofull widdows cries.

Tis He that doth behold thy inward cares,
And will regard the sorrowes of thy Soule;   50
Tis He that guides thy feet from Sathans snares,
And in his Wisedome, doth thy waies controule:
He through afflictions, still thy Minde prepares,
And all thy glorious Trialls will enroule:
   That when darke daies of terror shall appeare,   55
   Thou as the Sunne shalt shine; or much more cleare.

The Heav'ns shall perish as a garment olde,
Or as a vesture by the maker chang'd,
And shall depart, as when a skrowle is rolde;
Yet thou from him shalt never be estrang'd,   60
When He shall come in glory, that was solde
For all our sinnes; we happily are chang'd,
   Who for our faults put on his righteousnesse,
   Although full oft his Lawes we doe transgresse.

Long mai'st thou joy in this almightie love,   65
Long may thy Soule be pleasing in his sight,

Line 54. **Trialls**: sufferings.   **enroule**: enroll, keep track of.
Line 58. **vesture**: outward garment.   Line 59. **skrowle**: scroll.

Long mai'st thou have true comforts from above,
Long mai'st thou set on him thy whole delight,
And patiently endure when he doth prove,
Knowing that He will surely do thee right: 70
    Thy patience, faith, long suffring, and thy love,
    He will reward with comforts from above.

With Majestie and Honour is He clad,
And deck'd with light, as with a garment faire;
He joyes the Meeke, and makes the Mightie sad,   75
Pulls downe the Prowd, and doth the Humble reare:
Who sees this Bridegroome, never can be sad;
None lives that can his wondrous workes declare:
    Yea, looke how farre the Est is from the West,
    So farre he sets our sinnes that have transgrest.   80

He rides upon the wings of all the windes,
And spreads the heav'ns with his all powrefull hand;
Oh! who can loose when the Almightie bindes?
Or in his angry presence dares to stand?
He searcheth out the secrets of all mindes;   85
All those that feare him, shall possesse the Land:
    He is exceeding glorious to behold,
    Antient of Times; so faire, and yet so old.

Line 76. **reare**: raise up.

Line 77. **Bridegroome**: standard reference to Christ as the bridegroom or husband/
protector of the Christian soul and church generally, based on Christ's parable of the
bridegroom (Mat. 25:1–13) and the spiritualized Christian interpretation of the
sensuous wedding poetry in the Song of Solomon (also known as the Song of Songs, or
Canticles).

Lines 79–80. **farre ... transgrest**: Ps. 103:11–12. Direct echoes of the Psalms are
peppered throughout this poem, but especially in lines 73–144 (e.g. Ps. 97:5).

Line 80. **transgrest**: offended.

He of the watry Cloudes his Chariot frames,
And makes his blessed Angels powrefull Spirits,   90
His Ministers are fearefull fiery flames,
Rewarding all according to their merits;
The Righteous for an heritage he claimes,
And registers the wrongs of humble spirits:
    Hills melt like wax, in presence of the Lord,   95
    So do all sinners, in his sight abhorr'd.

He in the waters laies his chamber beames,
And cloudes of darkenesse compasse him about,
Consuming fire shall goe before in streames,
And burne up all his en'mies round about: 100
Yet on these Judgements worldlings never dreames,
Nor of these daungers never stand in doubt:
    While he shall rest within his holy Hill,
    That lives and dies according to his Will.

But woe to them that double-hearted bee,   105
Who with their tongues the righteous Soules doe slay;
Bending their bowes to shoot at all they see,
With upright hearts their Maker to obay;
And secretly doe let their arrowes flee,
To wound true hearted people any way: 110

Line 91. **Ministers**: those who do God's bidding.

Line 92. **Rewarding ... merits**: an exploitation of Old Testament themes of justice, since Protestant Christianity emphasized that salvation came by faith, not merit. The righteous elect were nonetheless allowed to take comfort from the Psalmist's insistence on God's ultimate determination to set right the worldly wrongs His chosen people suffered.

Line 98. **compasse**: encompass.

The Lord wil roote them out that speak prowd things,
Deceitfull tongues are but false Slanders wings.

Froward are the ungodly from their berth,
No sooner borne, but they doe goe astray;
The Lord will roote them out from off the earth,   115
And give them to their en'mies for a pray,
As venemous as Serpents is their breath,
With poysned lies to hurt in what they may
    The Innocent: who as a Dove shall flie
    Unto the Lord, that he his cause may trie.   120

The righteous Lord doth righteousnesse allow,
His countenance will behold the thing that's just;
Unto the Meane he makes the Mightie bow,
And raiseth up the Poore out of the dust:
Yet makes no count to us, nor when, nor how,   125
But powres his grace on all, that puts their trust
    In him: that never will their hopes betray,
    Nor lets them perish that for mercie pray.

He shall within his Tabernacle dwell,
Whose life is uncorrupt before the Lord,   130
Who no untrueths of Innocents doth tell,
Nor wrongs his neighbour, nor in deed, nor word,
Nor in his pride with malice seems to swell,

Line 113. **Froward**: contrary, recalcitrant; inclined to evil.
Line 116. **pray**: prey, victim.   Line 120. **trie**: prove by testing.
Line 123. **Meane**: lowly.   Line 129. **Tabernacle**: temple, place of holy repose.

Nor whets his tongue more sharper than a sword,
   To wound the reputation of the Just; 135
   Nor seekes to lay their glorie in the Dust.

That great *Jehova* King of heav'n and earth,
Will raine downe fire and brimstone from above,
Upon the wicked monsters in their berth
That storme and rage at those whom he doth love: 140
Snares, stormes, and tempests he will raine,
     and dearth,
Because he will himselfe almightie prove:
   And this shall be their portion they shall drinke,
   That thinkes the Lord is blind when he doth winke.

Pardon (good Madame) though I have digrest 145
From what I doe intend to write of thee,
To set his glorie forth whom thou lov'st best,
Whose wondrous works no mortall eie can see;
His speciall care on those whom he hath blest
From wicked worldlings, how he sets them free: 150
   And how such people he doth overthrow
   In all their waies, that they his powre may know.

The meditation of this Monarchs love,
Drawes thee from caring what this world can yield;
Of joyes and griefes both equall thou dost prove, 155
They have no force, to force thee from the field:

To the
Countesse of
Cumberland.

Line 134. **whets:** sharpens.

Line 139. **in ... berth:** where they reside.   Line 141. **dearth:** scarcity.

Lines 153–54. **meditation ... yield:** the "digression" of lines 73–144 has been designed
to comfort the Countess in her worldly troubles.

Thy constant faith like to the Turtle Dove
Continues combat, and will never yield
　　To base affliction; or prowd pomps desire,
　　That sets the weakest mindes so much on fire.　　　160

Thou from the Court to the Countrie art retir'd,
Leaving the world, before the world leaves thee:
That great Enchantresse of weake mindes admir'd,
Whose all-bewitching charmes so pleasing be
To worldly wantons; and too much desir'd　　　165
Of those that care not for Eternitie:
　　But yeeld themselves as preys to Lust and Sinne,
　　Loosing their hopes of Heav'n Hell paines to winne.

But thou, the wonder of our wanton age
Leav'st all delights to serve a heav'nly King:　　　170
Who is more wise? or who can be more sage,
Than she that doth Affection subject bring;
Not forcing for the world, or Satans rage,
But shrowding under the Almighties wing;
　　Spending her yeares, moneths, daies,
　　　　minutes, howres,　　　175
　　In doing service to the heav'nly powres.

Thou faire example, live without compare,
With Honours triumphs seated in thy breast;
Pale Envy never can thy name empaire,
When in thy heart thou harbour'st such a guest:　　　180
Malice must live for ever in dispaire;

Line 157. **Turtle Dove**: symbol of steadfast love.
Line 165. **wantons**: lewd and unrestrained people.

There's no revenge where Virtue still doth rest:
    All hearts must needs do homage unto thee,
    In whom all eies such rare perfection see.

That outward Beautie which the world commends,   185
Is not the subject I will write upon,
Whose date expir'd, that tyrant Time soone ends;
Those gawdie colours soone are spent and gone:
But those faire Virtues which on thee attends
Are alwaies fresh, they never are but one: 190
    They make thy Beautie fairer to behold,
    Than was that Queenes for whom prowd *Troy*
        was sold.

An Invective against outward beuty unaccompanied with virtue.

As for those matchlesse colours Red and White,
Or perfit features in a fading face,
Or due proportion pleasing to the sight;   195
All these doe draw but dangers and disgrace:
A mind enrich'd with Virtue, shines more bright,
Addes everlasting Beauty, gives true grace,
    Frames an immortall Goddesse on the earth,
    Who though she dies, yet Fame gives her new berth. 200

That pride of Nature which adornes the faire,
Like blasing Comets to allure all eies,
Is but the thred, that weaves their web of Care,
Who glories most, where most their danger lies;
For greatest perills do attend the faire,   205
When men do seeke, attempt, plot and devise,

Line 192. **that Queenes**: Helen of Troy; her beauty supposedly sparked the Trojan wars.

How they may overthrow the chastest Dame,
Whose Beautie is the White whereat they aime.

Twas Beautie bred in *Troy* the ten yeares strife,
And carried *Hellen* from her lawfull Lord;   210
Twas Beautie made chaste *Lucrece* loose her life,
For which prowd *Tarquins* fact was so abhorr'd:
Beautie the cause *Antonius* wrong'd his wife,
Which could not be decided but by sword:
    Great *Cleopatraes* Beautie and defects   215
    Did worke *Octaviaes* wrongs, and his neglects.

What fruit did yeeld that faire forbidden tree,
But blood, dishonour, infamie, and shame?
Poore blinded Queene, could'st thou no better see,
But entertaine disgrace, in stead of fame?   220
Doe these designes with Majestie agree?
To staine thy blood, and blot thy royall name.
    That heart that gave consent unto this ill,
    Did give consent that thou thy selfe should'st kill.

Line 208. **White ... aime**: breast of the deer, at which the hunter would aim his arrow; the deer hunt was a common metaphor for the chase of courtly love.

Line 210. **lawfull Lord**: the Greek king Menelaus, to whom Helen was married when she was abducted by the Trojan prince, Paris.

Line 211. **Lucrece**: Roman wife raped by the king's son, Sextus Tarquinius. She reported the rape, then committed suicide; an outraged revolt against the king's family introduced the Roman Republic. The story was familiar from Shakespeare's non-dramatic version (1593) and Thomas Heywood's play, *The Rape of Lucrece* (1608).

Line 213. **Antonius**: Marc Antony, one of three rulers of Rome (with Octavius and Lepidus), c. 42 B.C. He married Octavius's sister Octavia, then slighted her in favor of the Egyptian Queen Cleopatra, which provoked war with Octavius and led to Antony's suicide in 30 B.C.

Line 217. **forbidden tree**: the sin of adultery (Antony with Cleopatra).

Line 219. **blinded Queene**: Cleopatra, figuratively blind to the destruction her beauty was wreaking on Antony. She also committed suicide in 30 B.C.

Faire *Rosamund*, the wonder of her time,   225
Had bin much fairer, had shee not bin faire;
Beautie betraid her thoughts, aloft to clime,
To build strong castles in uncertaine aire,
Where th'infection of a wanton crime
Did worke her fall; first poyson, then despaire,   230
   With double death did kill her perjur'd soule,
   When heavenly Justice did her sinne controule.

                                                       Of
                                               Rosamund.

Holy *Matilda* in a haplesse houre
Was borne to sorow and to discontent,
Beauty the cause that turn'd her Sweet to Sowre,   235
While Chastity sought Folly to prevent.
Lustfull King *John* refus'd, did use his powre,
By Fire and Sword, to compasse his content:
   But Friends disgrace, nor Fathers banishment,
   Nor Death it selfe, could purchase her consent.   240

Of
Matilda.

Here Beauty in the height of all perfection,
Crown'd this faire Creatures everlasting fame,
Whose noble minde did scorne the base subjection
Of Feares, or Favours, to impaire her Name:
By heavenly grace, she had such true direction,   245
To die with Honour, not to live in Shame;
   And drinke that poyson with a cheerefull heart,
   That could all Heavenly grace to her impart.

Line 225. **Rosamund:** (d. 1176) mistress of King Henry II, said to have been poisoned by Queen Eleanor of Aquitaine. The story was familiar from Samuel Daniel's *Complaint of Rosamond* (1592).

Line 229. **wanton:** lustful.

Line 233. **Matilda:** virtuous maiden lustfully pursued by King John, as told for example by Michael Drayton in *Matilda* (1594).

*To the
Ladie of
Cumberland
the Intro-
duction to
the passion
of Christ.*

This Grace great Lady, doth possesse thy Soule,
And makes thee pleasing in thy Makers sight;   250
This Grace doth all imperfect Thoughts controule,
Directing thee to serve thy God aright;
Still reckoning him, the Husband of thy Soule,
Which is most pretious in his glorious sight:
    Because the Worlds delights shee doth denie   255
    For him, who for her sake vouchsaf'd to die.

And dying made her Dowager of all;
Nay more, Co-heire of that eternall blisse
That Angels lost, and We by *Adams* fall;
Meere Cast-awaies, rais'd by a *Judas* kisse,   260
Christs bloody sweat, the Vineger, and Gall,
The Speare, Sponge, Nailes, his buffeting with Fists,
    His bitter Passion, Agony, and Death,
    Did gaine us Heaven when He did loose his breath.

*A preamble
of the
Author
before the
Passion.*

These high deserts invites my lowely Muse   265
To write of Him, and pardon crave of thee,
For Time so spent, I need make no excuse,
Knowing it doth with thy faire Minde agree
So well, as thou no Labour wilt refuse,
    That to thy holy Love may pleasing be: 270

Line 251. **controule**: contain, restrict.

Line 257. **Dowager ... all**: though her husband's will deprived her of her widow's, or dowager lands, the Countess's soul gains her "all."

Lines 258–64. **eternall ... breath**: Lanyer here compresses the story of the fall of angels and humankind through disobedience to God, and the redemption Christ effected through his passion, or sufferings.

Line 265. **high deserts**: the purity of the Countess and the sacrifice of Christ. **deserts**: deservings.

His Death and Passion I desire to write,
And thee to reade, the blessed Soules delight.

But my deare Muse, now whither wouldst thou flie,
Above the pitch of thy appointed straine?
With *Icarus* thou seekest now to trie,   275
Not waxen wings, but thy poore barren Braine,
Which farre too weake, these siely lines descrie;
Yet cannot this thy forward Mind restraine,
    But thy poore Infant Verse must soare aloft,
    Not fearing threat'ning dangers, happening oft.   280

Thinke when the eye of Wisdom shall discover
Thy weakling Muse to flie, that scarce could creepe,
And in the Ayre above the Clowdes to hover,
When better 'twere mued up, and fast asleepe;
They'l thinke with *Phaeton*, thou canst neare recover,   285
But helplesse with that poore yong Lad to weepe:
    The little World of thy weake Wit on fire,
    Where thou wilt perish in thine owne desire.

But yet the Weaker thou doest seeme to be
In Sexe, or Sence, the more his Glory shines,   290
That doth infuze such powerfull Grace in thee,
To shew thy Love in these few humble Lines;

Line 275. **Icarus**: in Greek myth, son of the artist Daedalus. When he flew too close
to the sun on wax wings crafted by his father, the wings melted, and he fell to the sea.

Line 277. **siely**: silly, simple.   **descrie**: proclaim.

Line 278. **forward**: ambitious.   Line 284. **mued up**: confined, enclosed.

Line 285. **Phaeton**: reckless charioteer son of the Greek sun god Helios.

Line 290. **his**: Christ's.

The Widowes Myte, with this may well agree,
Her little All more worth than golden mynes,
   Beeing more deerer to our loving Lord,   295
   Than all the wealth that Kingdoms could affoard.

Therefore I humbly for his Grace will pray,
That he will give me Power and Strength to Write,
That what I have begun, so end I may,
As his great Glory may appeare more bright;   300
Yea in these Lines I may no further stray,
Than his most holy Spirit shall give me Light:
   That blindest Weakenesse be not over-bold,
   The manner of his Passion to unfold.

In other Phrases than may well agree   305
With his pure Doctrine, and most holy Writ,
That Heavens cleare eye, and all the World may see,
I seeke his Glory, rather than to get
The Vulgars breath, the seed of Vanitie,
Nor Fames lowd Trumpet care I to admit;   310
   But rather strive in plainest Words to showe,
   The Matter which I seeke to undergoe.

A Matter farre beyond my barren skill,
To shew with any Life this map of Death,

Line 293. **Widowes Myte**: in the parable, a widow gave all she had, though small, to the Temple in Jerusalem, while wealthier people gave less (Mark 12:41–44; Luke 21:1–4).

Lines 301–2. **Yea … Light**: her ability to write depends on grace given by God (through "his most holy Spirit"). See also lines 319–24.

Line 309. **Vulgars breath**: common people's praise.

Line 312. **undergoe**: undertake, present.

This Storie; that whole Worlds with Bookes would fill,   315
In these few Lines, will put me out of breath,
To run so swiftly up this mightie Hill,
I may behold it with the eye of Faith;
　　But to present this pure unspotted Lambe,
　　I must confesse, I farre unworthy am.   320

Yet if he please t'illuminate my Spirit,
And give me Wisdom from his holy Hill,
That I may Write part of his glorious Merit,
If he vouchsafe to guide my Hand and Quill,
To shew his Death, by which we doe inherit   325
Those endlesse Joyes that all our hearts doe fill;
　　Then will I tell of that sad blacke fac'd Night,
　　Whose mourning Mantle covered Heavenly Light.

That very Night our Saviour was betrayed,   *Here*
Oh night! exceeding all the nights of sorow,   330   *begins the*
When our most blessed Lord, although dismayed,   *Passion of*
Yet would not he one Minutes respite borrow,   *Christ.*
But to *Mount Olives* went, though sore afraid,
To welcome Night, and entertaine the Morrow;
　　And as he oft unto that place did goe,   335
　　So did he now, to meete his long nurst woe.

He told his deere Disciples that they all
Should be offended by him, that selfe night,
His Griefe was great, and theirs could not be small,

Line 328. **mourning Mantle**: dark cloak.

Line 333. **Mount Olives**: hill just outside Jerusalem. The story of the passion formally
begins here (see Introduction, page xxxiv).

To part from him who was their sole Delight;   340
Saint *Peter* thought his Faith could never fall,
No mote could happen in so cleare a sight:
    Which made him say, though all men
      were offended,
    Yet would he never, though his life were ended.

But his deare Lord made answere, That before   345
The Cocke did crowe, he should deny him thrice;
This could not choose but grieve him very sore,
That his hot Love should proove more cold than Ice,
Denying him he did so much adore;
No imperfection in himselfe he spies,   350
    But faith againe, with him hee'l surely die,
    Rather than his deare Master once denie.

And all the rest (did likewise say the same)
Of his Disciples, at that instant time;
But yet poore *Peter*, he was most too blame,   355
That thought above them all, by Faith to clime;
His forward speech inflicted sinne and shame,
When Wisdoms eyes did looke and checke his crime:
    Who did foresee, and told it him before,
    Yet would he needs averre it more and more.   360

Line 342. **mote**: obscuring blemish.   Line 358. **Wisdoms**: Christ's.

Line 360. **he ... more**: Peter kept insisting he would not deny Christ, which he later did, just as Jesus had predicted.   **averre**: aver, assert.

Now went our Lord unto that holy place,
Sweet *Gethsemaine* hallowed by his presence,
That blessed Garden, which did now embrace
His holy corps, yet could make no defence
Against those Vipers, objects of disgrace,   365
Which sought that pure eternall Love to quench:
    Here his Disciples willed he to stay,
    Whilst he went further, where he meant to pray.

None were admitted with their Lord to goe,
But *Peter*, and the sonnes of *Zebed'us*,   370
To them good *Jesus* opened all his woe,
He gave them leave his sorows to discusse,
His deepest griefes, he did not scorne to showe
These three deere friends, so much he did intrust:
    Beeing sorowfull, and overcharg'd with griefe,   375
    He told it them, yet look'd for no reliefe.

Sweet Lord, how couldst thou thus to flesh and blood
Communicate thy griefe? tell of thy woes?
Thou knew'st they had no powre to doe thee good,
But were the cause thou must endure these blowes,   380
Beeing the Scorpions bred in *Adams* mud,
Whose poys'ned sinnes did worke among thy foes,

Line 362. **Gethsemaine**: the Garden of Gethsemane, where Jesus spent his last night in prayer. He was attended by only three disciples—Peter, James, and John (Mat. 26:46, John 18:1).   **hallowed**: made holy.

Line 364. **corps**: body (living).   Line 370. **sonnes ... Zebed'us**: James and John.

Line 380. **were ... cause**: since Christ's sacrifice was offered to save humanity, no humans could intercede to help him.

To re-ore-charge thy over-burd'ned soule,
Although the sorowes now they doe condole.

Yet didst thou tell them of thy troubled state,   385
Of thy Soules heavinesse unto the death,
So full of Love, so free wert thou from hate,
To bid them stay, whose sinnes did stop thy breath,
When thou wert entring at so straite a gate,
Yea entring even into the doore of Death,   390
    Thou bidst them tarry there, and watch with thee,
    Who from thy pretious blood-shed were not free.

Bidding them tarry, thou didst further goe,
To meet affliction in such gracefull sort,
As might moove pitie both in friend and foe,   395
Thy sorowes such, as none could them comport,
Such great Indurements who did ever know,
When to th' Almighty thou didst make resort?
    And falling on thy face didst humbly pray,
    If 'twere his Will that Cup might passe away.   400

Saying, Not my will, but thy will Lord be done.
When as thou prayedst an Angel did appeare
From Heaven, to comfort thee Gods onely Sonne,
That thou thy Suffrings might'st the better beare,

Line 383. **re-ore-charge**: overcharge, or overburden, again.

Line 389. **straite**: narrow.   Line 391. **tarry**: linger.

Line 392. **Who ... free**: Jesus's chief disciples, along with the rest of humankind, inherited the sin that could only be purged by the blood of Christ's sacrifice.

Line 396. **comport**: endure.   Line 397. **Indurements**: endurances.

Line 400. **that Cup**: death by crucifixion (Mat. 26:43).

Beeing in an agony, thy glasse neere run, 405
Thou prayedst more earnestly, in so great feare,
   That pretious sweat came trickling to the ground,
   Like drops of blood thy sences to confound.

Loe here his Will, not thy Will, Lord was done,
And thou content to undergoe all paines, 410
Sweet Lambe of God, his deare beloved Sonne,
By this great purchase, what to thee remaines?
Of Heaven and Earth thou hast a Kingdom wonne,
Thy Glory beeing equall with thy Gaines,
   In ratifying Gods promise on the Earth, 415
   Made many hundred yeares before thy birth.

But now returning to thy sleeping Friends,
That could not watch one houre for love of thee,
Even those three Friends, which on thy Grace depends,
Yet shut those Eies that should their Maker see; 420
What colour, what excuse, or what amends,
From thy Displeasure now can set them free?
   Yet thy pure Pietie bids them Watch and Pray,
   Lest in Temptation they be led away.

Lines 405. **glasse neere run**: time nearly run out (as in an hourglass).

Line 408. **blood**: Luke 22:43–44.

Line 409. **his ... Will**: the will of God the father (not the will of Jesus, as Christ the son).

Line 411. **Lambe of God**: Christ.

Line 415. **Gods promise**: reference to Christian belief that many Old Testament stories forecast God's promise that his people would be saved.

Line 419. **which**: who.   Line 421. **colour**: reason.

Although the Spirit was willing to obay,   425
Yet what great weakenesse in the Flesh was found!
They slept in Ease, whilst thou in Paine didst pray;
Loe, they in Sleepe, and thou in Sorow drown'd:
Yet Gods right Hand was unto thee a stay,
When horror, griefe, and sorow did abound: 430
 His Angel did appeare from Heaven to thee,
 To yeeld thee comfort in Extremitie.

But what could comfort then thy troubled Minde,
When Heaven and Earth were both against thee bent?
And thou no hope, no ease, no rest could'st finde,   435
But must restore that Life, which was but lent;
Was ever Creature in the World so kinde,
But he that from Eternitie was sent?
 To satisfie for many Worlds of Sinne,
 Whose matchlesse Torments did but then begin.   440

If one Mans sinne doth challendge Death and Hell,
With all the Torments that belong thereto:
If for one sinne such Plagues on *David* fell,
As grieved him, and did his Seed undoe:

Lines 425–26. **Spirit ... Flesh**: paraphrase of Mat. 26:41.

Line 429. **stay**: support. Line 432. **Extremitie**: the end of life.

Line 437. **so kinde**: of humankind, so truly human.

Line 443. **Plagues on David**: when David did a census of his people against God's wishes, they suffered a great plague (1 Chron. 21:1–17).

If *Salomon*, for that he did not well,   445
Falling from Grace, did loose his Kingdome too:
    Ten Tribes beeing taken from his wilfull Sonne
    And Sinne the Cause that they were all undone.

What could thy Innocency now expect,
When all the Sinnes that ever were committed,   450
Were laid to thee, whom no man could detect?
Yet farre thou wert of Man from beeing pittied,
The Judge so just could yeeld thee no respect,
Nor would one jot of penance be remitted;
    But greater horror to thy Soule must rise,   455
    Than Heart can thinke, or any Wit devise.

Now drawes the houre of thy affliction neere,
And ugly Death presents himselfe before thee;
Thou now must leave those Friends thou held'st so deere,
Yea those Disciples, who did most adore thee;   460
Yet in thy countenance doth no Wrath appeare,
Although betrayd to those that did abhorre thee:
    Thou did'st vouchsafe to visit them againe,
    Who had no apprehension of thy paine.

Their eyes were heavie, and their hearts asleepe,   465
Nor knew they well what answere then to make thee;

Lines 445–47. **Salomon ... Sonne:** Solomon's son Rehoboam lost most of his father's kingdom; instead of taking good counsel, he added to "the heavy yoke" that the people felt Solomon had "put upon us" (2 Chron. 10).

Line 451. **detect:** expose as guilty.

Line 463. **vouchsafe:** see fit.   Line 464. **apprehension:** perception.

Yet thou as Watchman, had'st a care to keepe
Those few from sinne, that shortly would forsake thee;
But now thou bidst them henceforth Rest and Sleepe,
Thy houre is come, and they at hand to take thee: 470
 The Sonne of God to Sinners made a pray,
 Oh hatefull houre! oh blest! oh cursed day!

Loe here thy great Humility was found,
Beeing King of Heaven, and Monarch of the Earth,
Yet well content to have thy Glory drownd,   475
By beeing counted of so meane a berth;
Grace, Love, and Mercy did so much abound,
Thou entertaindst the Crosse, even to the death:
 And nam'dst thy selfe, the sonne of Man to be,
 To purge our pride by thy Humilitie.   480

But now thy friends whom thou didst call to goe,
Heavy Spectators of thy haplesse case,
See thy Betrayer, whom too well they knowe,
One of the twelve, now object of disgrace,
A trothlesse traytor, and a mortall foe,   485
With fained kindnesse seekes thee to imbrace;
 And gives a kisse, whereby he may deceive thee,
 That in the hands of Sinners he might leave thee.

Line 470. **they:** soldiers. Line 478. **entertaindst:** accepted, endured

Line 479. **sonne of Man:** term for the messiah, or savior.

Line 482. **Heavy:** sad, despondent. **haplesse:** unlucky, hopeless.

Line 483. **thy Betrayer:** Judas Iscariot, one of the twelve principal disciples.

Line 485. **trothlesse:** disloyal, untrustworthy. Line 486. **fained:** pretended.

Now muster forth with Swords, with Staves, with Bils,
High Priests and Scribes, and Elders of the Land,   490
Seeking by force to have their wicked Wils,
Which thou didst never purpose to withstand;
Now thou mak'st haste unto the worst of Ils,
And who they seeke, thou gently doest demand;
　　This didst thou Lord, t'amaze these Fooles the more, 495
　　T'inquire of that, thou knew'st so well before.

When loe these Monsters did not shame to tell,
His name they sought, and found, yet could not know
Jesus of Nazareth, at whose feet they fell,
When Heavenly Wisdome did descend so lowe   500
To speake to them: they knew they did not well,
Their great amazement made them backeward goe:
　　Nay, though he said unto them, I am he,
　　They could not know him, whom their eyes did see.

How blinde were they could not discerne the Light!   505
How dull! if not to understand the truth,
How weake! if meekenesse overcame their might;
How stony hearted, if not mov'd to ruth:
How void of Pitie, and how full of Spight,
Gainst him that was the Lord of Light and Truth: 510
　　Here insolent Boldnesse checkt by Love and Grace,
　　Retires, and falls before our Makers face.

Line 489. **Staves**: large sticks, used as weapons.　**Bils**: axe-like weapons.
Line 492. **purpose**: intend.
Lines 494–96. **who ... before**: Jesus anticipates their confrontation (John 18:4–8).
Line 506. **dull**: slow-witted.　Line 508. **ruth**: pity, regret.

For when he spake to this accursed crew,
And mildely made them know that it was he:
Presents himselfe, that they might take a view;   515
And what they doubted they might cleerely see;
Nay more, to re-assure that it was true,
He said: I say unto you, I am hee.
 If him they sought, he's willing to obay,
 Onely desires the rest might goe their way.   520

Thus with a heart prepared to endure
The greatest wrongs Impietie could devise,
He was content to stoope unto their Lure,
Although his Greatnesse might doe otherwise:
Here Grace was seised on with hands impure,   525
And Virtue now must be supprest by Vice,
 Pure Innocencie made a prey to Sinne,
 Thus did his Torments and our Joyes beginne.

Here faire Obedience shined in his breast,
And did suppresse all feare of future paine;   530
Love was his Leader unto this unrest,
Whil'st Righteousnesse doth carry up his Traine;
Mercy made way to make us highly blest,
When Patience beat downe Sorrow, Feare and Paine:
 Justice sate looking with an angry brow,   535
 On blessed misery appeering now.

More glorious than all the Conquerors
That ever liv'd within this Earthly round,

Line 528. **his … Joyes**: because his death on the cross made freedom from sin, and everlasting life, possible for humankind.

More powrefull than all Kings, or Governours
That ever yet within this World were found;   540
More valiant than the greatest Souldiers
That ever fought, to have their glory crown'd:
    For which of them, that ever yet tooke breath,
    Sought t'indure the doome of Heaven and Earth?

But our sweet Saviour whom these Jewes did name;   545
Yet could their learned Ignorance apprehend
No light of grace, to free themselves from blame:
Zeale, Lawes, Religion, now they doe pretend
Against the truth, untruths they seeke to frame:
Now al their powres, their wits, their strengths,
      they bend   550
    Against one siely, weake, unarmed man,
    Who no resistance makes, though much he can,

To free himselfe from these unlearned men,
Who call'd him Saviour in his blessed name;
Yet farre from knowing him their Saviour then,   555
That came to save both them and theirs from blame;
Though they retire and fall, they come agen
To make a surer purchase of their shame:
    With lights and torches now they find the way,
    To take the Shepheard whilst the sheep doe stray.   560

Why should unlawfull actions use the Light?
Inniquitie in Darkenesse seekes to dwell;
Sinne rides his circuit in the dead of Night,

Line 551. **siely**: simple, innocent.

Teaching all soules the ready waies to hell;
Sathan coms arm'd with all the powres of Spight,   565
Heartens his Champions, makes them rude and fell;
　　Like rav'ning wolves, to shed his guiltlesse blood,
　　Who thought no harme, but di'd to doe them good.

Here Falshood beares the shew of formall Right,
Base Treacherie hath gote a guard of men;   570
Tyranny attends, with all his strength and might,
To leade this siely Lamb to Lyons denne;
Yet he unmoov'd in this most wretched plight,
Goes on to meete them, knowes the houre, and when:
　　The powre of darkenesse must expresse Gods ire,   575
　　Therefore to save these few was his desire.

These few that wait on Poverty and Shame,
And offer to be sharers in his Ils;
These few that will be spreaders of his Fame,
He will not leave to Tyrants wicked wils;   580
But still desires to free them from all blame,
Yet Feare goes forward, Anger Patience kils:
　　A Saint is mooved to revenge a wrong,
　　And Mildnesse doth what doth to Wrath belong.

For *Peter* griev'd at what might then befall,   585
Yet knew not what to doe, nor what to thinke,
Thought something must be done; now, if at all,
To free his Master, that he might not drinke
This poys'ned draught, farre bitterer than gall,

Line 566. **rude**: barbarous.　**fell**: fierce, savage.　Line 589. **gall**: bile, bitterness.

For now he sees him at the very brinke   590
   Of griesly Death, who gins to shew his face,
   Clad in all colours of a deepe disgrace.

And now those hands, that never us'd to fight,
Or drawe a weapon in his owne defence,
Too forward is, to doe his Master right,   595
Since of his wrongs, hee feeles so true a sence:
But ah poore *Peter!* now thou wantest might,
And hee's resolv'd, with them he will goe hence:
   To draw thy sword in such a helpelesse cause,
   Offends thy Lord, and is against the Lawes.   600

So much he hates Revenge, so farre from Hate,
That he vouchsafes to heale, whom thou dost wound;
His paths are Peace, with none he holdes Debate,
His Patience stands upon so sure a ground,
To counsell thee, although it comes too late: 605
Nay, to his foes, his mercies so abound,
   That he in pitty doth thy will restraine,
   And heales the hurt, and takes away the paine.

For willingly he will endure this wrong,
Although his pray'rs might have obtain'd such grace,   610
As to dissolve their plots though ne'r so strong,
And bring these wicked Actors in worse case

Line 599. **draw thy sword**: one of the disciplines, described as Peter in John 18:10, cut off the ear of the high priest's servant (Mat. 26:51–52, Mark 14:47, Luke 22:50–51). In the Luke version, Jesus healed the wound.

Than *Ægypts* King on whom Gods plagues did throng,
But that foregoing Scriptures must take place:
   If God by prayers had an army sent   615
   Of powrefull Angels, who could them prevent?

Yet mightie JESUS meekely ask'd, Why they
With Swords and Staves doe come as to a Thiefe?
Hee teaching in the Temple day by day
None did offend, or give him cause of griefe.   620
Now all are forward, glad is he that may
Give most offence, and yeeld him least reliefe:
   His hatefull foes are ready now to take him,
   And all his deere Disciples do forsake him.

Those deare Disciples that he most did love,   625
And were attendant at his becke and call,
When triall of affliction came to prove,
They first left him, who now must leave them all:
For they were earth, and he came from above,
Which made them apt to flie, and fit to fall: 630
   Though they protest they never will forsake him,
   They do like men, when dangers overtake them.

And he alone is bound to loose us all,
Whom with unhallowed hands they led along,

Line 613. **Ægypts … throng**: allusion to biblical account of the plagues which God
brought upon Egypt for holding the Israelites in slavery (Ex. 7–13).

Line 614. **foregoing Scriptures**: biblical prophecies.

Line 630. **apt … fall**: suitable to fly and tending to fall.

Line 633. **bound**: tied up.   **loose**: set free (with pun on "bound").

To wicked *Caiphas* in the Judgement Hall,   635
Who studies onely how to doe him wrong;
High Priests and Elders, People great and small,
With all reprochfull words about him throng:
    False Witnesses are now call'd in apace,
    Whose trothlesse tongues must make pale
        death imbrace   640

The beauty of the World, Heavens chiefest Glory;
The mirrour of Martyrs, Crowne of holy Saints;
Love of th'Almighty, blessed Angels story;
Water of Life, which none that drinks it, faints;
Guide of the Just, where all our Light we borrow;   645
Mercy of Mercies; Hearer of Complaints;
    Triumpher over Death; Ransomer of Sinne;
    Falsly accused: now his paines begin.

Their tongues doe serve him as a Passing bell,
For what they say is certainly beleeved;   650
So sound a tale unto the Judge they tell,
That he of Life must shortly be bereaved;
Their share of Heaven, they doe not care to sell,
So his afflicted Heart be throughly grieved:
    They tell his Words, though farre from his intent,   655
    And what his Speeches were, not what he meant.

Line 635. **Caiphas**: high priest of Jerusalem who tried Christ for blasphemy.
Line 639. **apace**: swiftly.   Line 640. **trothlesse**: untruthful.   Line 644. **faints**: dies.
Line 649. **Their tongues**: those of the false witnesses.   Line 652. **bereaved**: robbed.

That he Gods holy Temple could destroy,
And in three daies could build it up againe;
This seem'd to them a vaine and idle toy,
It would not sinke into their sinful braine: 660
Christs blessed body, al true Christians joy,
Should die, and in three dayes revive againe:
   This did the Lord of Heaven and earth endure,
   Unjustly to be charg'd by tongues impure.

And now they all doe give attentive eare,   665
To heare the answere, which he will not make;
The people wonder how he can forbeare,
And these great wrongs so patiently can take;
But yet he answers not, nor doth he care,
Much more he will endure for our sake: 670
   Nor can their wisdoms any way discover,
   Who he should be that proov'd so true a Lover.

To entertaine the sharpest pangs of death,
And fight a combate in the depth of hell,
For wretched Worldlings made of dust and earth,   675
Whose hard'ned hearts, with pride and mallice swell;
In midst of bloody sweat, and dying breath,
He had compassion on these tyrants fell:
   And purchast them a place in Heav'n for ever,
   When they his Soule and Body sought to sever.   680

Lines 657–58. **he ... againe:** the witnesses report Christ's metaphorical prophecy of his own death and resurrection as if it were literal (John 2:19–21; Mat. 26:61).

Line 659. **toy:** foolish notion.

Sinnes ugly mists, so blinded had their eyes,
That at Noone dayes they could discerne no Light;
These were those fooles, that thought themselves so wise,
The Jewish wolves, that did our Saviour bite;
For now they use all meanes they can devise,   685
To beate downe truth, and goe against all right:
    Yea now they take Gods holy name in vaine,
    To know the truth, which truth they doe prophane.

The chiefest Hel-hounds of this hatefull crew,
Rose up to aske what answere he could make,   690
Against those false accusers in his view;
That by his speech, they might advantage take:
He held his peace, yet knew they said not true,
No answere would his holy wisdome make,
    Till he was charged in his glorious name,   695
    Whose pleasure 'twas he should endure this shame.

Then with so mild a Majestie he spake,
As they might easly know from whence he came,
His harmelesse tongue doth no exceptions take,
Nor Priests, nor People, meanes he now to blame;   700
But answers Folly, for true Wisdomes sake,
Beeing charged deeply by his powrefull name,
    To tell if Christ the Sonne of God he be,
    Who for our sinnes must die, to set us free.

Line 689. **chiefest Hel-hounds**: high priests (Mat. 26:62).

To thee O *Caiphas* doth he answere give,   705
That thou hast said, what thou desir'st to know,
And yet thy malice will not let him live,
So much thou art unto thy selfe a foe;
He speaketh truth, but thou wilt not beleeve,
Nor canst thou apprehend it to be so: 710
    Though he expresse his Glory unto thee,
    Thy Owly eies are blind, and cannot see.

Thou rend'st cloathes, in stead of thy false heart,
And on the guiltlesse lai'st thy guilty crime;
For thou blasphem'st, and he must feele the smart: 715
To sentence death, thou think'st it now high time;
No witnesse now thou need'st, for this fowle part,
Thou to the height of wickednesse canst clime:
    And give occasion to the ruder sort,
    To make afflictions, sorrows, follies sport.   720

Now when the dawne of day gins to appeare,
And all your wicked counsels have an end,
To end his Life, that holds you all so deere,
For to that purpose did your studies bend;
Proud *Pontius Pilate* must the matter heare,   725
To your untroths his eares he now must lend:

Lines 705–6. **To … know**: you have said what you wished to know (Caiphas, asking whether Christ is the son of God, has answered his own question). See Mark 14:60–63.

Line 710. **apprehend**: perceive.

Line 713. **Thou … heart**: you tear your clothes (a conventional sign of penitence) instead of opening your heart (to the words of the son of God).

Sweet *Jesus* bound, to him you led away,
Of his most pretious blood to make your pray.

Which, when that wicked Caytife did perceive,
By whose lewd meanes he came to this distresse;   730
He brought the price of blood he did receive,
Thinking thereby to make his fault seeme lesse,
And with these Priests and Elders did it leave,
Confest his fault, wherein he did transgresse:
    But when he saw Repentance unrespected,   735
    He hang'd himselfe; of God and Man rejected.

By this Example, what can be expected
From wicked Man, which on the Earth doth live?
But faithlesse dealing, feare of God neglected;
Who for their private gaine cares not to sell   740
The Innocent Blood of Gods most deere elected,
As did that caytife wretch, now damn'd in Hell:
    If in Christs Schoole, he tooke so great a fall,
    What will they doe, that come not there at all.

Now *Pontius Pilate* is to judge the Cause   745
Of faultlesse *Jesus*, who before him stands;
Who neither hath offended Prince, nor Lawes,
Although he now be brought in woefull bands:
O noble Governour, make thou yet a pause,
Doe not in innocent blood imbrue thy hands;   750

Line 728. **pray**: prey.   Line 729. **Caytife**: literally, slave; a reference to Judas.

Line 736. **He hang'd himselfe**: Mat. 27:3–75.

Line 745. **Pontius Pilate**: Roman governor of Jerusalem 26–36 A.D. and the final word in capital cases.

But heare the words of thy most worthy wife,
Who sends to thee, to beg her Saviours life.

Let barb'rous crueltie farre depart from thee,
And in true Justice take afflictions part;
Open thine eies, that thou the truth mai'st see,   755
Doe not the thing that goes against thy heart,
Condemne not him that must thy Saviour be;
But view his holy Life, his good desert.
    Let not us Women glory in Mens fall,
    Who had power given to over-rule us all.   760

Eves   Till now your indiscretion sets us free,
Apologie.   And makes our former fault much lesse appeare;
Our Mother *Eve*, who tasted of the Tree,
Giving to *Adam* what shee held most deare,
Was simply good, and had no powre to see,   765
The after-comming harme did not appeare:
    The subtile Serpent that our Sex betraide,
    Before our fall so sure a plot had laide.

That undiscerning Ignorance perceav'd
No guile, or craft that was by him intended;   770
For had she knowne, of what we were bereav'd,
To his request she had not condiscended.

Lines 751–52. **heare ... life**: what follows expands extensively on Mat. 27:19: "When [Pilate] was set down on the judgment seat, his wife sent unto him, saying, Have you nothing to do with that just man: for I have suffered many things this day in a dream because of him."

Lines 761–62. **Till ... appeare**: now your (men's) lack of judgment (in condemning Jesus) frees women by making Eve's fall to temptation seem much less by comparison (cf. Gen. 3:1–7).

Line 767. **subtile**: crafty.   Line 770. **him**: the serpent.

But she (poore soule) by cunning was deceav'd,
No hurt therein her harmelesse Heart intended:
 For she alleadg'd Gods word, which he denies,   775
 That they should die, but even as Gods, be wise.

But surely *Adam* can not be excusde,
Her fault though great, yet hee was most too blame;
What Weaknesse offerd, Strength might have refusde,
Being Lord of all, the greater was his shame: 780
Although the Serpents craft had her abusde,
Gods holy word ought all his actions frame,
 For he was Lord and King of all the earth,
 Before poore *Eve* had either life or breath.

Who being fram'd by Gods eternall hand,   785
The perfect'st man that ever breath'd on earth;
And from Gods mouth receiv'd that strait command,
The breach whereof he knew was present death:
Yea having powre to rule both Sea and Land,
Yet with one Apple wonne to loose that breath   790
 Which God had breathed in his beauteous face,
 Bringing us all in danger and disgrace.

And then to lay the fault on Patience backe,
That we (poore women) must endure it all;
We know right well he did discretion lacke,   795
Beeing not perswaded thereunto at all;

Line 775. **alleadg'd**: put forward (that is, she resisted the serpent's argument).
Line 779. **Weaknesse**: Eve. **Strength**: Adam.
Lines 783–84. **he ... breath**: Gen. 2:7–22.
Line 793. **Patience**: Eve and women generally. Line 795. **discretion**: judgment.

If *Eve* did erre, it was for knowledge sake,
The fruit beeing faire perswaded him to fall:
　　No subtill Serpents falshood did betray him,
　　If he would eate it, who had powre to stay him?   800

Not *Eve*, whose fault was onely too much love,
Which made her give this present to her Deare,
That what shee tasted, he likewise might prove,
Whereby his knowledge might become more cleare;
He never sought her weakenesse to reprove,   805
With those sharpe words, which he of God did heare:
　　Yet Men will boast of Knowledge, which he tooke
　　From *Eves* faire hand, as from a learned Booke.

If any Evill did in her remaine,
Beeing made of him, he was the ground of all;   810
If one of many Worlds could lay a staine
Upon our Sexe, and worke so great a fall
To wretched Man, by Satans subtill traine,
What will so fowle a fault amongst you all?
　　Her weakenesse did the Serpents words obay;   815
　　But you in malice Gods deare Sonne betray.

Whom, if unjustly you condemne to die,
Her sinne was small, to what you doe commit;
All mortall sinnes that doe for vengeance crie,
Are not to be compared unto it: 820
If many worlds would altogether trie,

Line 800. **stay**: stop.　Line 803. **prove**: test.

Line 810. **Beeing … him**: Gen. 2:21–23.　Line 813. **traine**: trickery.

Line 819. **mortall sinnes**: the most terrible violations of God's order, risking damnation.

By all their sinnes the wrath of God to get;
　　This sinne of yours, surmounts them all as farre
　　As doth the Sunne, another little starre.

Then let us have our Libertie againe,　　　　　　825
And challendge to your selves no Sov'raigntie;
You came not in the world without our paine,
Make that a barre against your crueltie;
Your fault beeing greater, why should you disdaine
Our beeing your equals, free from tyranny?　　　830
If one weake woman simply did offend,
　This sinne of yours, hath no excuse, nor end.

To which (poore soules) we never gave consent,
Witnesse thy wife (O *Pilate*) speakes for all;
Who did but dreame, and yet a message sent,　　835
That thou should'st have nothing to doe at all
With that just man; which, if thy heart relent,
Why wilt thou be a reprobate with *Saul?*
　　To seeke the death of him that is so good,
　　For thy soules health to shed his dearest blood.　　840

Yea, so thou mai'st these sinful people please,
Thou art content against all truth and right,
To seale this act, that may procure thine ease
With blood, and wrong, with tyrannie, and might;
The multitude thou seekest to appease,　　　　845

Line 826. **challendge**: attribute, claim.

Line 838. **Why ... Saul**: first king of Israel, rejected by God for disobedience, who plotted to kill his successor, David (1 Sam. 22–23). (Alternatively, another Saul, who later converted and changed his name to Paul, and who was a notorious early persecutor of the first Christians [Acts 9:1–31].)

By base dejection of this heavenly Light:
    Demanding which of these that thou should'st loose,
    Whether the Thiefe, or Christ King of the Jewes.

Base *Barrabas* the Thiefe, they all desire,
And thou more base than he, perform'st their will;   850
Yet when thy thoughts backe to themselves retire,
Thou art unwilling to commit this ill:
Oh that thou couldst unto such grace aspire,
That thy polluted lips might never kill
    That Honour, which right Judgement ever graceth,   855
    To purchase shame, which all true worth defaceth.

Art thou a Judge, and asketh what to do
With one, in whom no fault there can be found?
The death of Christ wilt thou consent unto,
Finding no cause, no reason, nor no ground?   860
Shall he be scourg'd, and crucified too?
And must his miseries by thy meanes abound?
    Yet not asham'd to aske what he hath done,
    When thine owne conscience seeks this sinne
        to shunne.

Three times thou ask'st, What evill hath he done?   865
And saist, thou find'st in him no cause of death,
Yet wilt thou chasten Gods beloved Sonne,
Although to thee no word of ill he saith:
For Wrath must end, what Malice hath begunne,
And thou must yield to stop his guiltlesse breath.   870

Line 846. **dejection**: humiliation.
Line 849. **Barrabas**: criminal released instead of Jesus (Mat. 27:16–26).

This rude tumultuous rowt doth presse so sore,
That thou condemnest him thou shouldst adore.

Yet *Pilate*, this can yeeld thee no content,
To exercise thine owne authoritie,
But unto *Herod* he must needes be sent,   875
To reconcile thy selfe by tyrannie:
Was this the greatest good in Justice meant,
When thou perceiv'st no fault in him to be?
    If thou must make thy peace by Virtues fall,
    Much better 'twere not to be friends all.   880

Yet neither thy sterne browe, nor his great place,
Can draw an answer from the Holy One:
His false accusers, nor his great disgrace,
Nor *Herods* scoffes; to him they are all one:
He neither cares, nor feares his owne ill case,   885
Though being despis'd and mockt of every one:
    King *Herods* gladnesse gives him little ease,
    Neither his anger seekes he to appease.

Yet this is strange, that base Impietie
Should yeeld those robes of honour, which were due;   890
Pure white, to shew his great Integritie,

Line 871. **rowt**: crowd.

Line 873. **Yet Pilate**: here or in the next stanza the voice of Pilate's wife probably merges back into the narrative voice.

Line 875. **Herod**: King of Judea; he and Pilate were enemies who became reconciled over Christ's death (see lines 879–80; Luke 23:12).

Line 881. **great place**: Herod's kingship.

Line 890. **robes of honour**: Herod's soldiers mockingly dressed Jesus in scarlet robes, a color only royalty was permitted to wear. See also, the "Crowne of Thornes," line 897 (Mat. 27:28–29).

His innocency, that all the world might view;
Perfections height in lowest penury,
Such glorious poverty as they never knew:
    Purple and Scarlet well might him beseeme,   895
    Whose pretious blood must all the world redeeme.

And that Imperiall Crowne of Thornes he wore,
Was much more pretious than the Diadem
Of any King that ever liv'd before,
Or since his time, their honour's but a dreame   900
To his eternall glory, beeing so poore,
To make a purchasse of that heavenly Realme;
    Where God with all his Angels lives in peace,
    No griefes, nor sorrowes, but all joyes increase.

Those royall robes, which they in scorne did give,   905
To make him odious to the common sort,
Yeeld light of Grace to those whose soules shall live
Within the harbour of this heavenly port;
Much doe they joy, and much more doe they grieve,
His death, their life, should make his foes such sport: 910
    With sharpest thornes to pricke his blessed face,
    Our joyfull sorrow, and his greater grace.

Three feares at once possessed *Pilates* heart;
The first, Christs innocencie, which so plaine appeares;
The next, That he which now must feele this smart,   915
Is Gods deare Sonne, for any thing he heares:
But that which proov'd the deepest wounding dart,

Line 916. **any … heares**: Pilate hears all rumors, including one that Jesus may be
"God's deare Sonne."

Is Peoples threat'nings, which he so much feares,
   That he to *Cæsar* could not be a friend,
   Unlesse he sent sweet JESUS to his end.   920

Now *Pilate* thou art proov'd a painted wall,
A golden Sepulcher with rotten bones;
From right to wrong, from equitie to fall:
If none upbraid thee, yet the very stones
Will rise against thee, and in question call   925
His blood, his teares, his sighes, his bitter groanes:
   All these will witnesse at the latter day,
   When water cannot wash thy sinne away.

Canst thou be innocent, that gainst all right,
Wilt yeeld to what thy conscience doth withstand?   930
Beeing a man of knowledge, powre, and might,
To let the wicked carrie such a hand,
Before thy face to blindfold Heav'ns bright light,
And thou to yeeld to what they did demand?
   Washing thy hands, thy conscience cannot cleare,   935
   But to all worlds this staine must needs appeare.

For loe, the Guiltie doth accuse the Just,
And faultie Judge condemnes the Innocent;
And wilfull Jewes to exercise their lust,
With whips and taunts against their Lord are bent;   940
He basely used, blasphemed, scorn'd and curst,
Our heavenly King to death for us they sent:

Line 935. **Washing ... hands**: Pilate tried to rid himself of guilt by publicly washing his hands and claiming himself innocent of "this man's blood" (Mat. 27:24).

Reproches, slanders, spittings in his face,
Spight doing all her worst in his disgrace.

Christ
going to
death.
And now this long expected houre drawes neere,   945
When blessed Saints with Angels doe condole;
His holy march, soft pace, and heavy cheere,
In humble sort to yeeld his glorious soule,
By his deserts the fowlest sinnes to cleare;
And in th'eternall booke of heaven to enroule   950
   A satisfaction till the generall doome,
   Of all sinnes past, and all that are to come.

They that had seene this pitifull Procession,
From *Pilates* Palace to Mount Calvarie,
Might thinke he answer'd for some great transgression,   955
Beeing in such odious sort condemn'd to die;
He plainely shewed that his own profession
Was virtue, patience, grace, love, piety:
   And how by suffering he could conquer more
   Than all the Kings that ever liv'd before.   960

First went the Crier with open mouth proclayming
The heavy sentence of Iniquitie,
The Hangman next, by his base office clayming
His right in Hell, where sinners never die,
Carrying the nayles, the people still blaspheming   965
Their maker, using all impiety;

Line 949. **deserts**: deservings (by his innocent self-sacrifice).

Line 951. **generall doome**: universal fate. God's final judgment of everyone at the end of the world; the apocalypse.

Line 956. **odious**: horrible.

The Thieves attending him on either side,
The Serjeants watching, while the women cri'd.

*The teares
of the
daughters
of
Jerusalem.*

Thrice happy women that obtaind such grace
From him whose worth the world could not containe;   970
Immediately to turne about his face,
As not remembring his great griefe and paine,
To comfort you, whose teares powr'd forth apace
On *Flora's* bankes, like shewers of Aprils raine:
    Your cries inforced mercie, grace, and love   975
    From him, whom greatest Princes could not moove:

To speake one word, nor once to lift his eyes
Unto proud *Pilate*, no nor *Herod*, king;
By all the Questions that they could devise,
Could make him answere to no manner of thing;   980
Yet these poore women, by their pitious cries
Did moove their Lord, their Lover, and their King,
    To take compassion, turne about, and speake
    To them whose hearts were ready now to breake.

Most blessed daughters of Jerusalem,   985
Who found such favour in your Saviors sight,
To turne his face when you did pitie him;
Your tearefull eyes, beheld his eies more bright;
Your Faith and Love unto such grace did clime,
To have reflection from this Heav'nly Light: 990

Line 969. **Thrice happy women**: the women who wept as they followed Jesus (Luke 23:27–31). Jesus' actual words to the women predict great disasters, but lines 985–92 suggest that his very speaking is a blessing.

Your Eagles eyes did gaze against this Sunne,
Your hearts did thinke, he dead, the world were done.

When spightfull men with torments did oppresse
Th'afflicted body of this innocent Dove,
Poore women seeing how much they did transgresse,   995
By teares, by sighes, by cries intreat, may prove,
What may be done among the thickest presse,
They labor still these tyrants hearts to move;
   In pitie and compassion to forbeare
    Their whipping, spurning, tearing of his haire.   1000

But all in vaine, their malice hath no end,
Their hearts more hard than flint, or marble stone;
Now to his griefe, his greatnesse they attend,
When he (God knowes) had rather be alone;
They are his guard, yet seeke all meanes to offend: 1005
Well may he grieve, well may he sigh and groane,
   Under the burthen of a heavy crosse,
    He faintly goes to make their gaine his losse.

The sorrow   His woefull Mother wayting on her Sonne,
of the   All comfortlesse in depth of sorow drowned;   1010
virgin   Her griefes extreame, although but new begun,
Marie.   To see his bleeding body oft shee swouned;
How could shee choose but thinke her selfe undone,
He dying, with whose glory shee was crowned?

Line 991. **Eagles eyes**: eagles were known for their excellent sight.   **Sunne**: popular pun on the "Son [of God]."

Line 1001. **their**: the "tyrants" of line 998; the chief priests and elders who refused to listen to the women.

None ever lost so great a losse as shee,   1015
  Beeing Sonne, and Father of Eternitie.

Her teares did wash away his pretious blood,
That sinners might not tread it under feet
To worship him, and that it did her good
Upon her knees, although in open street,   1020
Knowing he was the Jessie floure and bud,
That must be gath'red when it smell'd most sweet:
  Her Sonne, her Husband, Father, Saviour, King,
  Whose death killd Death, and tooke away his sting.

Most blessed Virgin, in whose faultlesse fruit,   1025
All Nations of the earth must needes rejoyce,
No Creature having sence though ne'r so brute,
But joyes and trembles when they heare his voyce;
His wisedome strikes the wisest persons mute,
Faire chosen vessell, happy in his choyce: 1030
  Deere Mother of our Lord, whose reverend name,
  All people Blessed call, and spread thy fame.

For the Almightie magnified thee,
And looked downe upon thy meane estate;
Thy lowly mind, and unstain'd Chastitie   1035
Did pleade for Love at great *Jehovaes* gate,
Who sending swift-wing'd *Gabriel* unto thee,
His holy will and pleasure to relate;

Line 1021. **floure ... bud**: Jesus as culmination and new man of his ancestral line.

Line 1025. **faultlesse fruit**: Christ.

Lines 1032–35. **Blessed ... Chastitie**: paraphrase of part of Mary's song of thanks, the Magnificat (Luke 1:48–49).

To thee most beauteous Queene of Woman-kind,
The Angell did unfold his Makers mind.   1040

He thus beganne, Haile *Mary* full of grace,
Thou freely art beloved of the Lord,
He is with thee, behold thy happy case;
What endlesse comfort did these words afford
To thee that saw'st an Angell in the place   1045
Proclaime thy Virtues worth, and to record
    Thee blessed among women: that thy praise
    Should last so many worlds beyond thy daies.

Loe, this high message to thy troubled spirit,
He doth deliver in the plainest sence;   1050
Sayes, Thou shouldst beare a Sonne that shal inherit
His Father *Davids* throne, free from offence,
Call's him that Holy thing, by whose pure merit
We must be sav'd, tels what he is, of whence;
    His worth, his greatnesse, what his name must be, 1055
    Who should be call'd the Sonne of the most High.

He cheeres thy troubled soule, bids thee not feare;
When thy pure thoughts could hardly apprehend
This salutation, when he did appeare;
Nor couldst thou judge, whereto those words
    did tend;   1060
His pure aspect did moove thy modest cheere

Lines 1041–48. **Haile Mary ... thy daies**: paraphrase of the Angel's greeting to Mary (Luke 1:28–30). Lines 1049–96 expand upon the encounter between Mary and the Angel in Luke 1:28–55.

To muse, yet joy that God vouchsaf'd to send
   His glorious Angel; who did thee assure
   To beare a child, although a Virgin pure.

Nay more, thy Sonne should Rule and Raigne
     for ever; 1065
Yea, of his Kingdom there should be no end;
Over the house of *Jacob*, Heavens great Giver
Would give him powre, and to that end did send
His faithfull servant *Gabriel* to deliver
To thy chast eares no word that might offend: 1070
   But that this blessed Infant borne of thee,
   Thy Sonne, The onely Sonne of God should be.

When on the knees of thy submissive heart
Thou humbly didst demand, How that should be?
Thy virgin thoughts did thinke, none could impart 1075
This great good hap, and blessing unto thee;
Farre from desire of any man thou art,
Knowing not one, thou art from all men free:
   When he, to answere this thy chaste desire,
   Gives thee more cause to wonder and admire. 1080

That thou a blessed Virgin shoulst remaine,
Yea that the holy Ghost should come on thee
A maiden Mother, subject to no paine,
For highest powre should overshadow thee:
Could thy faire eyes from teares of joy refraine, 1085

Line 1067. **house of Jacob**: Israel.
Line 1069. **Gabriel**: the Angel speaking to Mary.   Line 1076. **hap**: luck, fortune.

When God look'd downe upon thy poore degree?
    Making thee Servant, Mother, Wife, and Nurse
    To Heavens bright King, that freed us from the curse.

Thus beeing crown'd with glory from above,
Grace and Perfection resting in thy breast,   1090
Thy humble answer doth approove thy Love,
And all these sayings in thy heart doe rest:
Thy Child a Lambe, and thou a Turtle dove,
Above all other women highly blest;
    To find such favour in his glorious sight,   1095
    In whom thy heart and soule doe most delight.

What wonder in the world more strange could seeme,
Than that a Virgin could conceive and beare
Within her wombe a Sonne, That should redeeme
All Nations on the earth, and should repaire   1100
Our old decaies: who in such high esteeme,
Should prize all mortals, living in his feare;
    As not to shun Death, Povertie, and Shame,
    To save their soules, and spread his glorious Name.

And partly to fulfil his Fathers pleasure,   1105
Whose powrefull hand allowes it not for strange,
If he vouchsafe the riches of his treasure,
Pure Righteousnesse to take such il exchange;
On all Iniquitie to make a seisure,

Line 1086. **poore degree**: low estate, position.

Line 1088. **curse**: original sin (see Introduction, page xxxvii).

Line 1091. **approove**: prove.   Line 1093. **Turtle dove**: symbol for steadfast love.

Giving his snow-white Weed for ours in change   1110
   Our mortall garment in a skarlet Die,
   Too base a roabe for Immortalitie.

Most happy news, that ever yet was brought,
When Poverty and Riches met together,
The wealth of Heaven, in our fraile clothing wrought   1115
Salvation by his happy comming hither:
Mighty Messias, who so deerely bought
Us Slaves to sinne, farre lighter than a feather:
   Toss'd to and fro with every wicked wind,
   The world, the flesh, or Devill gives to blind.   1120

Who on his shoulders our blacke sinnes doth beare
To that most blessed, yet accursed Crosse;
Where fastning them, he rids us of our feare,
Yea for our gaine he is content with losse,
Our ragged clothing scornes he not to weare,   1125
Though foule, rent, torne, disgracefull, rough
      and grosse,
   Spunne by that monster Sinne, and weav'd by Shame,
   Which grace it selfe, disgrac'd with impure blame.

How canst thou choose (faire Virgin) then but mourne,
When this sweet of-spring of thy body dies,   1130

Line 1110. **Weed**: clothing. Here God is clothed in a spotless body.

Line 1111. **skarlet Die**: scarlet dye, blood.

Lines 1118–20. **lighter … blind**: fallen humans are like feathers blown around by the traditional sources of sin: the world, the flesh, and the devil.

Line 1126. **rent**: ragged.

When thy faire eies beholds his bodie torne,
The peoples fury, heares the womens cries;
His holy name prophan'd, He made a scorne,
Abusde with all their hatefull slaunderous lies:
 Bleeding and fainting in such wondrous sort,   1135
 As scarce his feeble limbes can him support.

Now *Simon* of *Cyrene* passeth them by,
Whom they compell sweet JESUS Crosse to beare
To *Golgatha*, there doe they meane to trie
All cruell meanes to worke in him dispaire: 1140
That odious place, where dead mens skulls did lie,
There must our Lord for present death prepare:
 His sacred blood must grace that loathsome field,
 To purge more filth, than that foule place could yield.

Christs
death.
For now arriv'd unto this hatefull place,   1145
In which his Crosse erected needes must bee,
False hearts, and willing hands come on apace,
All prest to ill, and all desire to see:
Gracelesse themselves, still seeking to disgrace;
Bidding him, If the Sonne of God he bee,   1150
 To save himselfe, if he could others save,
 With all th'opprobrious words that might deprave.

His harmelesse hands unto the Crosse they nailde,
And feet that never trode in sinners trace,
Betweene two theeves, unpitied, unbewailde,   1155

Line 1137. **Simon of Cyrene:** Mat. 27:32.

Line 1139. **Golgatha:** hill outside of Jerusalem, known as the "place of the skulls," where Jesus was crucified (Mat. 27:33).

Save of some few possessors of his grace,
With sharpest pangs and terrors thus appailde,
Sterne Death makes way, that Life might give him place:
　　His eyes with teares, his body full of wounds,
　　Death last of paines his sorrows all confounds.　　1160

His joynts dis-joynted, and his legges hang downe,
His alablaster breast, his bloody side,
His members torne, and on his head a Crowne
Of sharpest Thorns, to satisfie for pride:
Anguish and Paine doe all his Sences drowne,　　1165
While they his holy garments do divide:
　　His bowells drie, his heart full fraught with griefe,
　　Crying to him that yeelds him no reliefe.

This with the eie of Faith thou maist behold,
Deere Spouse of Christ, and more than I can write;　　1170
And here both Griefe and Joy thou maist unfold,
To view thy Love in this most heavy plight,
Bowing his head, his bloodlesse body cold;
Those eies waxe dimme that gave us all our light,
　　His count'nance pale, yet still continues sweet,　　1175
　　His blessed blood watring his pierced feet.

To my Ladie of Cumberland.

O glorious miracle without compare!
Last, but not least which was by him effected;
Uniting death, life, misery, joy and care,

Line 1157. **appailde**: dismayed or terrified; hemmed in, trapped.

Line 1163. **members**: body parts, limbs.

Line 1168. **Crying to him**: calling upon God.

Line 1170. **Spouse of Christ**: Margaret, Countess of Cumberland, representing the convention that the Christian soul is the bride of Christ.

By his sharpe passion in his deere elected:　　　　1180
Who doth the Badges of like Liveries weare,
Shall find how deere they are of him respected.
　　No joy, griefe, paine, life, death, was like to his,
　　Whose infinitie dolours wrought eternall blisse.

The terror What creature on the earth did then remaine,　　1185
of all On whom the horror of this shamefull deed
creatures Did not inflict some violent touch, or straine,
at that To see the Lord of all the world to bleed?
instant His dying breath did rend huge rockes in twaine,
when The heavens betooke them to their mourning weed:　　1190
Christ died. 　　The Sunne grew darke, and scorn'd to give
　　　　　them light,
　　　Who durst ecclipse a glory farre more bright.

The Moone and Starres did hide themselves for shame,
The earth did tremble in her loyall feare,
The Temple vaile did rent to spread his fame,　　　　1195
The Monuments did open every where;
Dead Saints did rise forth of their graves, and came
To divers people that remained there
　　Within that holy City; whose offence,
　　Did put their Maker to this large expence.　　　　1200

Line 1181. **Badges ... Liveries:** whoever wears the "badge" or emblem of pain and suffering will receive special understanding from Christ, who endured ultimate pain. A livery is a gift of distinctive clothing from master to servant.

Line 1184. **dolours:** sorrows.

Lines 1189–98. **His dying ... there:** Christ's death produced great omens of destruction (Mat. 27:51–53; Luke 23:45).

Things reasonable, and reasonlesse possest
The terrible impression of this fact;
For his oppression made them all opprest,
When with his blood he seal'd so faire an act,
In restlesse miserie to procure our rest;   1205
His glorious deedes that dreadfull prison sackt:
    When Death, Hell, Divells, using all their powre,
    Were overcome in that most blessed houre.

Being dead, he killed Death, and did survive
That prowd insulting Tyrant: in whose place   1210
He sends bright Immortalitie to revive
Those whom his yron armes did long embrace;
Who from their loathsome graves brings them alive
In glory to behold their Saviours face:
    Who tooke the keys of all Deaths powre away,   1215
    Opening to those that would his name obay.

O wonder, more than man can comprehend,
Our Joy and Griefe both at one instant fram'd,
Compounded: Contrarieties contend
Each to exceed, yet neither to be blam'd.   1220
Our Griefe to see our Saviours wretched end,
Our Joy to know both Death and Hell he tam'd:
    That we may say, O Death, where is thy sting?
    Hell, yeeld thy victory to thy conq'ring King.

Line 1202. **impression**: imprint.   Line 1206. **dreadfull prison**: death.
Line 1212. **his**: Death's.

Can stony hearts refraine from shedding teares,   1225
To view the life and death of this sweet Saint?
His austere course in yong and tender yeares,
When great indurements could not make him faint:
His wants, his paines, his torments, and his feares,
All which he undertooke without constraint,   1230
   To shew that infinite Goodnesse must restore,
    What infinite Justice looked for, and more.

Yet, had he beene but of a meane degree,
His suffrings had beene small to what they were;
Meane minds will shew of what meane mouldes
     they bee;   1235
Small griefes seeme great, yet Use doth make them beare:
But ah! tis hard to stirre a sturdy tree;
Great dangers hardly puts great minds in feare:
   They will conceale their griefes which mightie grow
    In their stout hearts untill they overflow.   1240

If then an earthly Prince may ill endure
The least of those afflictions which he bare,
How could this all-commaunding King procure
Such grievous torments with his mind to square,
Legions of Angells being at his Lure?   1245
He might have liv'd in pleasure without care:
   None can conceive the bitter paines he felt,
    When God and man must suffer without guilt.

Line 1228. **indurements**: trials.   Line 1233. **meane**: low.   Line 1236. **Use**: habit.
Line 1245. **Lure**: bidding.

Take all the Suffrings Thoughts can thinke upon,
In ev'ry man that this huge world hath bred;   1250
Let all those Paines and Suffrings meet in one,
Yet are they not a Mite to that he did
Endure for us: Oh let us thinke thereon,
That God should have his pretious blood so shed:
    His Greatnesse clothed in our fraile attire,   1255
    And pay so deare a ransome for the hire.

Loe, here was glorie, miserie, life and death,
An union of contraries did accord;
Gladnesse and sadnesse here had one berth,
This wonder wrought the Passion of our Lord,   1260
He suffring for all the sinnes of all th'earth,
No satisfaction could the world afford:
    But this rich Jewell, which from God was sent,
    To call all those that would in time repent.

Which I present (deare Lady) to your view,   1265
Upon the Crosse depriv'd of life or breath,
To judge if ever Lover were so true,
To yeeld himselfe unto such shamefull death:
Now blessed *Joseph* doth both beg and sue,
To have his body who possest his faith,   1270
    And thinkes, if he this small request obtaines,
    He wins more wealth than in the world remaines.

Line 1252. **Mite:** tiny amount.   Line 1256. **hire:** borrowing of human form.

Line 1269. **Joseph:** Joseph of Arimathea, who gave Jesus his tomb (Mat. 27:57–58); see lines 1277–79.   **sue:** petition.

Thus honourable *Joseph* is possest,
Of what his heart and soule so much desired,
And now he goes to give that body rest,   1275
That all his life, with griefes and paines was tired;
He finds a Tombe, a Tombe most rarely blest,
In which was never creature yet interred;
    There this most pretious body he incloses,
    Imbalmd and deckt with Lillies and with Roses.   1280

Loe here the Beautie of Heav'n and Earth is laid,
The purest coulers underneath the Sunne,
But in this place he cannot long be staid,
Glory must end what horror hath begun;
For he the furie of the Heavens obay'd,   1285
And now he must possesse what he hath wonne:
    The *Maries* doe with pretious balmes attend,
    But beeing come, they find it to no end.

For he is rize from Death t'Eternall Life,
And now those pretious oyntments he desires   1290
Are brought unto him, by his faithfull Wife
The holy Church; who in those rich attires,
Of Patience, Love, Long suffring, Voide of strife,
Humbly presents those oyntments he requires:
    The oyles of Mercie, Charitie, and Faith,   1295
    Shee onely gives that which no other hath.

Line 1287. **Maries:** Mary Magdalene and "the other Mary" (Mat. 28:1; Luke 23:55–24:3).   **balmes:** oils used to dress the body after death.

Lines 1290–92. **pretious ... Church:** the funeral ointments are treated as bridal gifts in the conventional metaphor of the marriage between Christ and his Church.

These pretious balmes doe heale his grievous wounds,
And water of Compunction washeth cleane
The soares of sinnes, which in our Soules abounds;
So faire it heales, no skarre is ever seene; 1300
Yet all the glory unto Christ redounds,
His pretious blood is that which must redeeme;
　　Those well may make us lovely in his sight,
　　But cannot save without his powrefull might.

*A briefe
description
of his
beautie
upon the
Canticles.*

This is that Bridegroome that appeares so faire, 1305
So sweet, so lovely in his Spouses sight,
That unto Snowe we may his face compare,
His cheekes like skarlet, and his eyes so bright
As purest Doves that in the rivers are,
Washed with milke, to give the more delight; 1310
　　His head is likened to the finest gold,
　　His curled lockes so beauteous to behold;

Blacke as a Raven in her blackest hew;
His lips like skarlet threeds, yet much more sweet
Than is the sweetest hony dropping dew, 1315
Or hony combes, where all the Bees doe meet;
Yea, he is constant, and his words are true,
His cheekes are beds of spices, flowers sweet;
　　His lips, like Lillies, dropping downe pure mirrhe,
　　Whose love, before all worlds we doe preferre. 1320

Side note. **Canticles:** Old Testament book of wedding poems, whose language is reflected in lines 1305–20; also known as Song of Songs or Song of Solomon.

Line 1301. **redounds:** returns.

Line 1314. **lips … threeds:** Song of Sol. 3:4; though the songs in the Canticles praise both male and female beauty, this simile in its Biblical context describes the bride.

Line 1319. **mirrhe:** fragrant gum; perfume.

Ah! give me leave (good Lady) now to leave
This taske of Beauty which I tooke in hand,
I cannot wade so deepe, I may deceave
My selfe, before I can attaine the land;
Therefore (good Madame) in your heart I leave   1325
His perfect picture, where it still shall stand,
    Deepely engraved in that holy shrine,
    Environed with Love and Thoughts divine.

There may you see him as a God in glory,
And as a man in miserable case;   1330
There may you reade his true and perfect storie,
His bleeding body there you may embrace,
And kisse his dying cheekes with teares of sorrow,
With joyfull griefe, you may intreat for grace;
    And all your prayers, and your almes-deeds   1335
    May bring to stop his cruell wounds that bleeds.

Oft times hath he made triall of your love,
And in your Faith hath tooke no small delight,
By Crosses and Afflictions he doth prove,
Yet still your heart remaineth firme and right;   1340
Your love so strong, as nothing can remove,
Your thoughts beeing placed on him both day
      and night,
    Your constant soule doth lodge betweene her brests,
    This Sweet of sweets, in which all glory rests.

Line 1335. **almes-deeds**: acts of charity.   Line 1339. **prove**: test.
Line 1343. **her**: the soul's.

Sometime h'appeares to thee in Shepheards weed,   1345
And so presents himselfe before thine eyes,
A good old man; that goes his flocke to feed;
Thy colour changes, and thy heart doth rise;
Thou call'st, he comes, thou find'st tis he indeed,
Thy Soule conceaves that he is truely wise: 1350
    Nay more, desires that he may be the Booke,
    Whereon thine eyes continually may looke.

Sometime imprison'd, naked, poore, and bare,
Full of diseases, impotent, and lame,
Blind, deafe, and dumbe, he comes unto his faire,   1355
To see if yet shee will remaine the same;
Nay sicke and wounded, now thou do'st prepare
To cherish him in thy dear Lovers name:
    Yea thou bestow'st all paines, all cost, all care,
    That may relieve him, and his health repaire.   1360

These workes of mercy are so sweete, so deare
To him that is the Lord of Life and Love,
That all thy prayers he vouchsafes to heare,
And sends his holy Spirit from above;
Thy eyes are op'ned, and thou seest so cleare,   1365
No worldly thing can thy faire mind remove;
    Thy faith, thy prayers, and his speciall grace
    Doth open Heav'n, where thou behold'st his face.

These are those Keyes Saint *Peter* did possesse,
Which with a Spirituall powre are giv'n to thee,   1370

Line 1345. **weed**: clothing.   Line 1369. **Keyes ... possesse**: keys to heaven.

To heale the soules of those that doe transgresse,
By thy faire virtues; which, if once they see,
Unto the like they doe their minds addresse,
Such as thou art, such they desire to be:
    If they be blind, thou giv'st to them their sight;   1375
    If deafe or lame, they heare, and goe upright.

Yea, if possest with any evill spirits,
Such powre thy faire examples have obtain'd
To cast them out, applying Christs pure merits,
By which they are bound, and of all hurt restrain'd: 1380
If strangely taken, wanting sence or wits,
Thy faith appli'd unto their soules so pain'd,
    Healeth all griefes, and makes them grow so strong,
    As no defects can hang upon them long.

Thou beeing thus rich, no riches do'st respect,   1385
Nor do'st thou care for any outward showe;
The proud that doe faire Virtues rules neglect,
Desiring place, thou sittest them belowe:
All wealth and honour thou do'st quite reject,
If thou perceiv'st that once it prooves a foe   1390
    To virtue, learning, and the powres divine,
    Thou mai'st convert, but never wilt incline

Line 1379. **applying ... pure merits**: the invocation of Christ's innocency and sacrifice was believed to overcome evil. In this and the previous stanza, the Countess is credited with apostolic healing powers.

Line 1381. **strangely taken**: overcome by confusion.

Lines 1392–93. **Thou ... disorder**: you are able to convert the wicked, but are never tempted by their wickedness.

To fowle disorder, or licentiousnesse
But in thy modest vaile do'st sweetly cover
The staines of other sinnes, to make themselves,   1395
That by this meanes thou mai'st in time recover
Those weake lost sheepe that did so long transgresse,
Presenting them unto thy deerest Lover;
   That when he brings them backe unto his fold,
   In their conversion then he may behold   1400

Thy beauty shining brighter than the Sunne,
Thine honour more than ever Monarke gaind,
Thy wealth exceeding his that Kingdomes wonne,
Thy Love unto his Spouse, thy Faith unfaind,
Thy Constancy in what thou hast begun,   1405
Till thou his heavenly Kingdom have obtaind;
   Respecting worldly wealth to be but drosse,
   Which, if abuz'd, doth proove the owners losse.

Great *Cleopatra's* love to *Anthony,*
Can no way be compared unto thine;   1410
Shee left her Love in his extremitie,
When greatest need should cause her to combine
Her force with his, to get the Victory:

Line 1393. **licentiousnesse**: lawlessness, lust.

Line 1397. **lost sheepe**: sinful souls, a common Christian metaphor (Mat. 9:36, 12:11–12).

Line 1404. **unfaind**: unfeigned, unpretended.

Line 1407. **drosse**: waste that results from melting metal; unrefinable material.

Line 1409. **Cleopatra's love**: the model of a great passion; see note to lines 213 and 219, above.

Lines 1411–13. **Shee ... Victory**: Cleopatra's ships abandoned the sea battle and left Antony's forces at the mercy of Octavius; their defeat provoked Antony's and then Cleopatra's suicides.

Her Love was earthly, and thy Love Divine;
   Her Love was onely to support her pride,   1415
   Humilitie thy Love and Thee doth guide.

That glorious part of Death, which last shee plai'd,
T'appease the ghost of her deceased Love,
Had never needed, if shee could have stai'd
When his extreames made triall, and did prove   1420
Her leaden love unconstant, and afraid:
Their wicked warres the wrath of God might move
   To take revenge for chast *Octavia's* wrongs,
   Because shee enjoyes what unto her belongs.

No *Cleopatra*, though thou wert as faire   1425
As any Creature in *Antonius* eyes;
Yea though thou wert as rich, as wise, as rare,
As any Pen could write, or Wit devise;
Yet with this Lady canst thou not compare,
Whose inward virtues all thy worth denies: 1430
   Yet thou a blacke Egyptian do'st appeare;
   Thou false, shee true; and to her Love more deere.

Shee sacrificeth to her deerest Love,
With flowres of Faith, and garlands of Good deeds;
Shee flies not from him when afflictions prove,   1435
Shee beares his crosse, and stops his wounds that bleeds;
Shee love and lives chaste as the Turtle dove,
Shee attends upon him, and his flocke shee feeds;

Line 1421. **leaden**: heavy, earth-bound.

Line 1424. **shee … her**: Cleopatra … Octavia.

Line 1429. **this Lady**: the Countess of Cumberland.

Yea for one touch of death which thou did'st trie,
A thousand deaths shee every day doth die. 1440

Her virtuous life exceeds thy worthy death,
Yea, she hath richer ornaments of state,
Shining more glorious than in dying breath
Thou didst; when either pride, or cruell fate,
Did worke thee to prevent a double death; 1445
To stay the malice, scorne, and cruell hate
   Of Rome; that joy'd to see thy pride pull'd downe,
   Whose Beauty wrought the hazard of her Crowne.

Good Madame, though your modestie be such,
Not to acknowledge what we know and find; 1450
And that you thinke these prayses overmuch,
Which doe expresse the beautie of your mind;
Yet pardon me although I give a touch
Unto their eyes, that else would be so blind,
   As not to see thy store, and their owne wants, 1455
   From whose faire seeds of Virtue spring
      these plants.

And knowe, when first into this world I came,
This charge was giv'n me by th'Eternall powres,
Th'everlasting Trophie of thy fame,
To build and decke it with the sweetest flowres 1460
That virtue yeelds; Then Madame, doe not blame
Me, when I shew the World but what is yours,

Line 1441. **Her ... thy:** the Countess's ... Cleopatra's.
Line 1447. **Of Rome:** of Octavius, the Roman victor over Cleopatra.

And decke you with that crowne which is your due,
That of Heav'ns beauty Earth may take a view.

Though famous women elder times have knowne,   1465
Whose glorious actions did appeare so bright,
That powrefull men by them were overthrowne,
And all their armies overcome in fight;
The Scythian women by their powre alone,
Put king *Darius* unto shamefull flight: 1470
   All Asia yeelded to their conq'ring hand,
   Great *Alexander* could not their powre withstand.

Whose worth, though writ in lines of blood and fire,
Is not to be compared unto thine;
Their powre was small to overcome Desire,   1475
Or to direct their wayes by Virtues line:
Were they alive, they would thy Life admire,
And unto thee their honours would resigne:
   For thou a greater conquest do'st obtaine,
   Than they who have so many thousands slaine.   1480

Wise *Deborah* that judged Israel,
Nor valiant *Judeth* cannot equall thee,
Unto the first, God did his will reveale,
And gave her powre to set his people free;

Line 1465. **elder:** former, ancient.

Line 1469–72. **Scythian ... withstand:** Alexander the Great (356–323 B.C.) conquered Darius, king of Persia, in 331 B.C.; Lanyer credits the women of Scythia with the conquest (see Sir Thomas North's translation of the story in Plutarch's *Lives*, 1579).

Line 1481. **Deborah:** one of the great judges of Israel (Judg. 4:4).

Line 1482. **Judeth:** heroine of the apocryphal book of Judith, who beheaded the enemy general, Holofernes (see line 1486).

Yea *Judeth* had the powre likewise to queale   1485
Proud *Holifernes*, that the just might see
    What small defence vaine pride, and greatnesse hath
    Against the weapons of Gods word and faith.

But thou farre greater warre do'st still maintaine,
Against that many headed monster Sinne,   1490
Whose mortall sting hath many thousand slaine,
And every day fresh combates doe begin;
Yet cannot all his venome lay one staine
Upon thy Soule, thou do'st the conquest winne,
    Though all the world he daily doth devoure,   1495
    Yet over thee he never could get powre.

For that one worthy deed by *Deb'rah* done,
Thou hast performed many in thy time;
For that one Conquest that faire *Judeth* wonne,
By which shee did the steps of honour clime;   1500
Thou hast the Conquest of all Conquests wonne,
When to thy Conscience Hell can lay no crime:
    For that one head that *Judeth* bare away,
    Thou tak'st from Sinne a hundred heads a day.

Though virtuous *Hester* fasted three dayes space,   1505
And spent her time in prayers all that while,
That by Gods powre shee might obtaine such grace,
That shee and hers might not become a spoyle
To wicked *Hamon*, in whose crabbed face

Line 1485. **queale**: quell.

Line 1505. **Hester**: Queen Esther, who interceded on behalf of her people, the Jews, and had their enemy Haman hanged (see line 1509; Esther 5–9).

Was seene the map of malice, envie, guile;   1510
   Her glorious garments though shee put apart,
   So to present a pure and single heart

To God, in sack-cloth, ashes, and with teares;
Yet must faire *Hester* needs give place to thee,
Who hath continu'd dayes, weekes, months,
     and yeares,   1515
In Gods true service, yet thy heart beeing free
From doubt of death, or any other feares:
Fasting from sinne, thou pray'st thine eyes may see
   Him that hath full possession of thine heart,
   From whose sweet love thy Soule can never part.   1520

His Love, not Feare, makes thee to fast and pray,
No kinsmans counsell needs thee to advise;
The sack-cloth thou do'st weare both night and day,
Is worldly troubles, which thy rest denies;
The ashes are the Vanities that play   1525
Over thy head, and steale before thine eyes;
   Which thou shak'st off when mourning time is past,
   That royall roabes thou may'st put on at last.

Joachims wife, that faire and constant Dame,
Who rather chose a cruel death to die,   1530
Than yeeld to those two Elders voide of shame,

Line 1513. **sack-cloth, ashes**: traditional signs of penitence; symbols of poverty and mortality.

Line 1525. **Vanities**: fantasies.

Line 1529. **Joachims wife**: Susanna, heroine of the apocryphal book of Daniel and Susanna, who resisted two lustful elders who then accused her; she was vindicated by the young prophet Daniel (lines 1530–36).

When both at once her chastitie did trie,
Whose Innocencie bare away the blame,
Untill th'Almighty Lord had heard her crie;
　　And rais'd the spirit of a Child to speake,   1535
　　Making the powrefull judged of the weake.

Although her virtue doe deserve to be
Writ by that hand that never purchas'd blame;
In holy Writ, where all the world may see
Her perfit life, and ever honoured name: 1540
Yet was she not to be compar'd to thee,
Whose many virtues doe increase thy fame:
　　For shee oppos'd against old doting Lust,
　　Who with lifes danger she did feare to trust.

But your chaste breast, guarded with strength of mind,   1545
Hates the imbracements of unchaste desires;
You loving God, live in your selfe confind
From unpure Love, your purest thoughts retires,
Your perfit sight could never be so blind,
To entertaine the old or yong desires   1550
　　Of idle Lovers; which the world presents,
　　Whose base abuses worthy minds prevents.

Even as the constant Lawrell, alwayes greene,
No parching heate of Summer can deface,
Nor pinching Winter ever yet was seene,   1555
Whose nipping frosts could wither, or disgrace:

Line 1539. **holy Writ**: the Bible.　Line 1541. **thee**: the Countess of Cumberland.
Line 1553. **Lawrell**: traditional symbol of victory and poetic fame, the laurel is an evergreen.

So you (deere Ladie) still remaine as Queene,
Subduing all affections that are base,
   Unalterable by the change of times,
   Not following, but lamenting others crimes.   1560

No feare of Death, or dread of open shame,
Hinders your perfect heart to give consent;
Nor loathsome age, whom Time could never tame
From ill designes, whereto their youth was bent;
But love of God, care to preserve your fame,   1565
And spend that pretious time that God hath sent,
   In all good exercises of the minde,
   Whereto your noble nature is inclin'd.

That Ethyopian Queene did gaine great fame,
Who from the Southerne world, did come to see   1570
Great *Salomon;* the glory of whose name
Had spread it selfe ore all the earth, to be
So great, that all the Princes thither came,
To be spectators of his royaltie:
   And this faire Queene of Sheba came from farre,   1575
   To reverence this new appearing starre.

From th'utmost part of all the Earth shee came,
To heare the Wisdom of this worthy King;
To trie if Wonder did agree with Fame,
And many faire rich presents did she bring: 1580

Line 1564. **ill designes**: evil plans.

Line 1569. **Ethyopian Queene**: the Queen of Sheba (line 1575), who traveled to see for herself the wisdom and riches of King Solomon (2 Sam. 10:1–13). She was greatly impressed, and she and Solomon exchanged respect and rich gifts before she returned to her country (lines 1585–92).

Yea many strange hard questions did shee frame,
All which were answer'd by this famous King:
    Nothing was hid that in her heart did rest,
    And all to proove this King so highly blest.

Here Majestie with Majestie did meete,   1585
Wisdome to Wisdome yeelded true content,
One Beauty did another Beauty greet,
Bounty to Bountie never could repent;
Here all distaste is troden under feet,
No losse of time, where time was so well spent   1590
    In virtuous exercises of the minde,
    In which this Queene did much contentment finde.

Spirits affect where they doe sympathize,
Wisdom desires Wisdome to embrace,
Virtue covets her like, and doth devize   1595
How she her friends may entertaine with grace;
Beauty sometime is pleas'd to feed her eyes,
With viewing Beautie in anothers face:
    Both good and bad in this point doe agree,
    That each desireth with his like to be.   1600

And this Desire did worke a strange effect,
To drawe a Queene forth of her native Land,
Not yeelding to the nicenesse and respect
Of woman-kind; shee past both sea and land,
All feare of dangers shee did quite neglect,   1605
Onely to see, to heare, and understand

Line 1593. **affect**: are drawn to each other.   Line 1603. **nicenesse**: fastidiousness.
Lines 1603–4. **respect … woman-kind**: retiring role of women.

That beauty, wisedome, majestie, and glorie,
That in her heart imprest his perfect storie.

Yet this faire map of majestie and might,
Was but a figure of thy deerest Love,   1610
Borne t'expresse that true and heavenly light,
That doth all other joyes imperfect prove;
If this faire Earthly starre did shine so bright,
What doth that glorious Sonne that is above?
   Who weares th'imperiall crowne of heaven
      and earth,   1615
   And made all Christians blessed in his berth.

If that small sparke could yeeld so great a fire,
As to inflame the hearts of many Kings
To come to see, to heare, and to admire
His wisdome, tending but to worldly things;   1620
Then much more reason have we to desire
That heav'nly wisedome, which salvation brings;
   The Sonne of righteousnesse, that gives true joyes,
   When all they fought for, were but Earthly toyes.

No travels ought th'affected soule to shunne,   1625
That this faire heavenly Light desires to see:
This King of kings to whom we all should runne,
To view his Glory and his Majestie;
He without whom we all had beene undone,
He that from Sinne and Death hath set us free,   1630

Line 1610. **figure**: prefiguring.   **thy … Love**: the Countess of Cumberland's love for Christ.
Line 1620. **His**: Solomon's.

And overcome Satan, the world, and sinne,
That by his merits we those joyes might winne.

Prepar'd by him, whose everlasting throne
Is plac'd in heaven, above the starrie skies,
Where he that sate, was like the Jasper stone, 1635
Who rightly knowes him shall be truely wise,
A Rainebow round about his glorious throne;
Nay more, those winged beasts so full of eies,
    That never cease to glorifie his Name,
    Who was, and will be, and is now the same. 1640

This is that great almightie Lord that made
Both heaven and earth, and lives for evermore;
By him the worlds foundation first was laid:
He fram'd the things that never were before:
The Sea within his bounds by him is staid, 1645
He judgeth all alike, both rich and poore:
    All might, all majestie, all love, all lawe
    Remaines in him that keepes all worlds in awe.

From his eternall throne the lightning came,
Thundrings and Voyces did from thence proceede; 1650
And all the creatures glorifi'd his name,
In heaven, in earth, and seas, they all agreed,
When loe that spotlesse Lambe so voyd of blame,
That for us di'd, whose sinnes did make him bleed:

Line 1635. **Jasper stone:** bright jewel (Rev. 4:3). Lines 1633–72 offer a visionary
description of the enthroned and judging Christ, based on the Book of Revelation.
Line 1638. **winged ... eies:** Rev. 4:9.

That true Physition that so many heales,   1655
Opened the Booke, and did undoe the Seales.

He onely worthy to undoe the Booke
Of our charg'd soules, full of iniquitie,
Where with the eyes of mercy he doth looke
Upon our weakenesse and infirmitie;   1660
This is that corner stone that was forsooke,
Who leaves it, trusts but to uncertaintie:
  This is Gods Sonne, in whom he is well pleased,
  His deere beloved, that his wrath appeased.

He that had powre to open all the Seales,   1665
And summon up our sinnes of blood and wrong,
He unto whom the righteous soules appeales,
That have bin martyrd, and doe thinke it long,
To whom in mercie he his will reveales,
That they should rest a little in their wrong,   1670
  Untill their fellow servants should be killed,
  Even as they were, and that they were fulfilled.

To the Lady
dowager of
Cumberland.

Pure thoughted Lady, blessed be thy choyce
Of this Almightie, everlasting King;
In thee his Saints and Angels doe rejoyce,   1675
And to their Heav'nly Lord doe daily sing
Thy perfect praises in their lowdest voyce;
And all their harpes and golden vials bring
  Full of sweet odours, even thy holy prayers
  Unto that spotlesse Lambe, that all repaires.   1680

Line 1656. **Booke ... Seales:** Rev. 5:1, 6:1 ff.

Of whom that Heathen Queene obtain'd such grace,
By honouring but the shadow of his Love,
That great Judiciall day to have a place,
Condemning those that doe unfaithfull prove;
Among the haplesse, happie is her case,   1685
That her deere Saviour spake for her behove;
    And that her memorable Act should be
    Writ by the hand of true Eternitie.

Yet this rare Phoenix of that worne-out age,
This great majesticke Queene comes short of thee,   1690
Who to an earthly Prince did then ingage
Her hearts desires, her love, her libertie,
Acting her glorious part upon a Stage
Of weaknesse, frailtie, and infirmity:
    Giving all honour to a Creature, due   1695
    To her Creator, whom shee never knew.

But loe, a greater thou hast sought and found
Than *Salomon* in all his royaltie;
And unto him thy faith most firmely bound
To serve and honour him continually;   1700
That glorious God, whose terror doth confound
All sinfull workers of iniquitie:
    Him hast thou truely served all thy life,
    And for his love, liv'd with the world at strife.

Lines 1681–82. **Heathen ... Love**: Sheba's honor of Solomon foreshadows the Countess of Cumberland's more powerful love of Christ.

Line 1683. **Judiciall day**: judgment day.   Line 1686. **behove**: need.

Line 1687. **memorable Act**: Queen of Sheba's honor of Solomon, which prefigures the love of Christ.

Line 1689–90. **Phoenix ... Queene**: Queen of Sheba.   Line 1695. **Creature**: Solomon.

To this great Lord, thou onely art affected,　　　　　1705
Yet came he not in pompe or royaltie,
But in an humble habit, base, dejected;
A King, a God, clad in mortalitie,
He hath thy love, thou art by him directed,
His perfect path was faire humilitie:　　　　　1710
　　Who being Monarke of heav'n, earth, and seas,
　　Indur'd all wrongs, yet no man did displease.

Then how much more art thou to be commended,
That seek'st thy love in lowly shepheards weed?
A seeming Trades-mans sonne, of none attended,　　　1715
Save of a few in povertie and need;
Poore Fishermen that on his love attended,
His love that makes so many thousands bleed:
　　Thus did he come, to trie our faiths the more,
　　Possessing worlds, yet seeming extreame poore.　　1720

The Pilgrimes travels, and the Shepheards cares,
He tooke upon him to enlarge our soules,
What pride hath lost, humilitie repaires,
For by his glorious death he us inroules
In deepe Characters, writ with blood and teares,　　　1725
Upon those blessed Everlasting scroules;
　　His hands, his feete, his body, and his face,
　　Whence freely flow'd the rivers of his grace.

Line 1705. **To ... affected**: you love only God.

Line 1712. **yet ... displease**: yet offended no one.

Line 1717. **Poore Fishermen**: the apostles Peter, James, and John.

Line 1724. **inroules**: enrolls.　　Line 1725. **Characters**: letters.

Line 1728. **rivers ... grace**: Christ's redeeming blood.

Sweet holy rivers, pure celestiall springs,
Proceeding from the fountaine of our life;   1730
Swift sugred currents that salvation brings,
Cleare christall streames, purging all sinne and strife,
Faire floods, where souls do bathe their snow-white
      wings,
Before they flie to true eternall life:
      Sweet Nectar and Ambrosia, food of Saints,   1735
      Which, whoso tasteth, never after faints.

This hony dropping dew of holy love,
Sweet milke, wherewith we weaklings are restored,
Who drinkes thereof, a world can never move,
All earthly pleasures are of them abhorred;   1740
This love made Martyrs many deaths to prove,
To taste his sweetnesse, whom they so adored:
      Sweetnesse that makes our flesh a burthen to us,
      Knowing it serves but onely to undoe us.

His sweetnesse sweet'ned all the sowre of death,   1745
To faithfull *Stephen* his appointed Saint;
Who by the river stones did loose his breath,
When paines nor terrors could not make him faint:
So was this blessed Martyr turn'd to earth,
To glorifie his soule by deaths attaint: 1750
      This holy Saint was humbled and cast downe,
      To winne in heaven an everlasting crowne.

Line 1729. **holy rivers:** Rev. 22:1
Line 1746. **Stephen:** the first Christian martyr, stoned for his faith (Acts 6–7).
Line 1750. **attaint:** stigma.

Whose face repleat with Majestie and Sweetnesse,
Did as an Angel unto them appeare,
That sate in Counsell hearing his discreetnesse,   1755
Seeing no change, or any signe of a feare;
But with a constant browe did there confesse
Christs high deserts, which were to him so deare:
    Yea when these Tyrants stormes did most oppresse,
    Christ did appeare to make his griefe the lesse.   1760

For beeing filled with the holy Ghost,
Up unto Heav'n he look'd with stedfast eies,
Where God appeared with his heavenly hoste
In glory to this Saint before he dies;
Although he could no Earthly pleasures boast,   1765
At Gods right hand sweet JESUS he espies;
    Bids them behold Heavens open, he doth see
    The Sonne of Man at Gods right hand to be.

Whose sweetnesse sweet'ned that short sowre of Life,
Making all bitternesse delight his taste,   1770
Yeelding sweet quietnesse in bitter strife,
And most contentment when he di'd disgrac'd;
Heaping up joyes where sorrows were most rife;
Such sweetnesse could not choose but be imbrac'd:
    The food of Soules, the Spirits onely treasure,   1775
    The Paradise of our celestiall pleasure.

This Lambe of God, who di'd, and was alive,
Presenting us the bread of life Eternall,

Line 1753. **repleat**: filled.　　Line 1755. **discreetnesse**: judgment.
Line 1762. **he**: Stephen.　　Line 1768. **Sonne of Man**: Jesus.

His bruised body powrefull to revive
Our sinking soules, out of the pit infernall;   1780
For by this blessed food he did contrive
A worke of grace, by this his gift externall,
　　With heav'nly Manna, food of his elected,
　　To feed their soules, of whom he is respected.

This wheate of Heaven the blessed Angells bread,   1785
Wherewith he feedes his deere adopted Heires;
Sweet foode of life that doth revive the dead,
And from the living takes away all cares;
To taste this sweet Saint *Laurence* did not dread,
The broyling gridyorne cool'd with holy teares: 1790
　　Yeelding his naked body to the fire,
　　To taste this sweetnesse, such was his desire.

Nay, what great sweetnesse did th'Apostles taste,
Condemn'd by Counsell, when they did returne;
Rejoycing that for him they di'd disgrac'd,   1795
Whose sweetnes made their hearts and soules so burne
With holy zeale and love most pure and chaste;
For him they sought from whome they might not turne:
　　Whose love made *Andrew* goe most joyfully,
　　Unto the Crosse, on which he meant to die.   1800

The Princes of th'Apostles were so filled
With the delicious sweetnes of his grace,
That willingly they yeelded to be killed,

Line 1789–91. **Saint Laurence**: martyr burned for his beliefs.

Line 1799. **Andrew**: apostle martyred by crucifixion.

Line 1801. **Princes … Apostles**: Peter and John the Baptist, whose deaths are referred to in lines 1815–16.

Receiving deaths that were most vile and base,
For his name sake, that all might be fulfilled.   1805
They with great joy all torments did imbrace:
    The ugli'st face that Death could ever yeeld,
    Could never feare these Champions from the field.

They still continued in their glorious fight,
Against the enemies of flesh and blood;   1810
And in Gods law did set their whole delight,
Suppressing evill, and erecting good:
Not sparing Kings in what they did not right;
Their noble Actes they seal'd with deerest blood:
    One chose the Gallowes, that unseemely death,   1815
    The other by the Sword did loose his breath.

His Head did pay the dearest rate of sin,
Yeelding it joyfully unto the Sword,
To be cut off as he had never bin,
For speaking truth according to Gods word,   1820
Telling king *Herod* of incestuous sin,
That hatefull crime of God and man abhorr'd:
    His brothers wife, that prowd licentious Dame,
    Cut off his Head to take away his shame.

Loe Madame, heere you take a view of those,   1825
Whose worthy steps you doe desire to tread,

Line 1815. **One ... Gallowes:** Peter, who was crucified upside down.

Line 1816. **other ... Sword:** John the Baptist, who was beheaded for accusing King Herod of incest (lines 1817–24).

Line 1821. **Telling:** accusing.

Deckt in those colours which our Saviour chose;
The purest colours both of White and Red,   *Colours of*
Their freshest beauties would I faine disclose,   *Confessors*
By which our Saviour most was honoured: 1830 *& Martirs.*
    But my weake Muse desireth now to rest,
    Folding up all their Beauties in your breast.

Whose excellence hath rais'd my sprites to write,
Of what my thoughts could hardly apprehend;
Your rarest Virtues did my soule delight,   1835
Great Ladie of my heart: I must commend
You that appeare so faire in all mens sight:
On your Deserts my Muses doe attend:
    You are the Articke Starre that guides my hand,
    All what I am, I rest at your command.   1840

FINIS

Line 1833. **sprites**: spirits.
Line 1839. **Articke Starre**: North, or Pole, Star (the mariner's guide).

The Description of Cooke-ham

Farewell (sweet *Cooke-ham*) where I first obtain'd
Grace from that Grace where perfit Grace remain'd;
And where the Muses gave their full consent,
I should have powre the virtuous to content:
Where princely Palace will'd me to indite,   5
The sacred Storie of the Soules delight.
Farewell (sweet Place) where Virtue then did rest,
And all delights did harbour in her breast:
Never shall my sad eies againe behold
Those pleasures which my thoughts did then unfold: 10
Yet you (great Lady) Mistris of that Place,
From whose desires did spring this worke of Grace;
Vouchsafe to thinke upon those pleasures past,
As fleeting worldly Joyes that could not last:
Or, as dimme shadowes of celestiall pleasures,   15
Which are desir'd above all earthly treasures.

Title. **Cooke-ham**: crown manor leased to the Countess of Cumberland's brother, William Russell of Thornhaugh, where the Countess resided periodically until 1605 or shortly after (see Introduction, xxiv, n. 26). See discussion of Lanyer's autobiographical claims in this poem, Introduction, xxxix.

Line 2. **Grace ... Grace ... Grace**: favor, noble person, god-given virtues.

Line 3. **Muses**: in Greek myth, nine sisters who represented and bestowed skill in arts and learning, including poetry and music.

Line 5. **indite**: write.

Line 6. **sacred Storie**: possibly the story of Christ's passion in the "Salve Deus" poem, or the story of this poem, or a reference to yet another poem.

Line 10. **unfold**: disclose.

Line 12. **worke of Grace**: this poem.

Line 15. **shadowes**: reflections, images.

Oh how (me thought) against you thither came,
Each part did seeme some new delight to frame!
The House receiv'd all ornaments to grace it,
And would indure no foulenesse to deface it.   20
The Walkes put on their summer Liveries,
And all things else did hold like similies:
The Trees with leaves, with fruits, with flowers clad,
Embrac'd each other, seeming to be glad,
Turning themselves to beauteous Canopies,   25
To shade the bright Sunne from your brighter eies:
The cristall Streames with silver spangles graced,
While by the glorious Sunne they were embraced:
The little Birds in chirping notes did sing,
To entertaine both You and that sweet Spring.   30
And *Philomela* with her sundry leyes,
Both You and that delightfull Place did praise.
Oh how me thought each plant, each floure, each tree
Set forth their beauties then to welcome thee:
The very Hills right humbly did descend,   35
When you to tread upon them did intend.
And as you set your feete, they still did rise,
Glad that they could receive so rich a prise.
The gentle Windes did take delight to bee
Among those woods that were so grac'd by thee.   40
And in sad murmure utterd pleasing sound,

Line 21. **Liveries**: uniforms.

Line 22. **similies**: comparisons (nature is presented as richly dressed and ready to serve the Countess of Cumberland, lines 21–75).

Line 31. **Philomela**: the nightingale. **leyes**: lays; songs.

Line 32. **delightfull Place**: acknowledges Cookham in the classical tradition of the lovely or delightful place, the *locus amoenus*.

Line 41. **sad**: serious, deep.

That Pleasure in that place might more abound:
The swelling Bankes deliver'd all their pride,
When such a *Phœnix* once they had espide.
Each Arbor, Banke, each Seate, each stately Tree,　　　45
Thought themselves honor'd in supporting thee.
The pretty Birds would oft come to attend thee,
Yet flie away for feare they should offend thee:
The little creatures in the Burrough by
Would come abroad to sport them in your eye;　　　50
Yet fearefull of the Bowe in your faire Hand,
Would runne away when you did make a stand.
Now let me come unto that stately Tree,
Wherein such goodly Prospects you did see;
That Oake that did in height his fellowes passe,　　　55
As much as lofty trees, low growing grasse:
Much like a comely Cedar streight and tall,
Whose beauteous stature farre exceeded all:
How often did you visite this faire tree,
Which seeming joyfull in receiving thee,　　　60
Would like a Palme tree spread his armes abroad,
Desirous that you there should make abode:
Whose faire greene leaves much like a comely vaile,
Defended *Phebus* when he would assaile:
Whose pleasing boughes did yeeld a coole fresh ayre,　　　65
Joying his happinesse when you were there.

Line 44. **Phoenix**: mythical resplendent and eternal bird; the Countess.

Line 49. **Burrough**: burrow.

Line 51. **Bowe in your faire Hand**: the Countess is figured as the goddess Diana.

Line 63. **comely vaile**: attractive covering.

Line 64. **Defended Phebus**: protected against the sun.

Where beeing seated, you might plainely see,
Hills, vales, and woods, as if on bended knee
They had appeard, your honour to salute,
Or to preferre some strange unlook'd for sute: 70
All interlac'd with brookes and christall springs,
A Prospect fit to please the eyes of Kings:
And thirteene shires appear'd all in your sight,
Europe could not affoard much more delight.
What was there then but gave you all content,   75
While you the time in meditation spent,
Of their Creators powre, which there you saw,
In all his Creatures held a perfit Law;
And in their beauties did you plaine descrie,
His beauty, wisdome, grace, love, majestie.   80
In these sweet woods how often did you walke,
With Christ and his Apostles there to talke;
Placing his holy Writ in some faire tree,
To meditate what you therein did see:
With *Moyses* you did mount his holy Hill,   85
To know his pleasure, and performe his Will.
With lovely *David* you did often sing,
His holy Hymnes to Heavens Eternall King.
And in sweet musicke did your soule delight,
To sound his prayses, morning, noone, and night.   90

Line 70. **preferre**: offer.   **sute**: request.

Line 73. **shires**: counties; the grounds of Cookham were on a hill with a wide view.

Line 78. **Law**: order.

Line 85. **Moyses ... Hill**: Moses spoke with God on a mountaintop (Ex. 24:13–18; 25–32:33).

Line 87. **David**: the psalmist.

With blessed *Joseph* you did often feed
Your pined brethren, when they stood in need.
And that sweet Lady sprung from *Cliffords* race,
Of noble *Bedfords* blood, faire steame of Grace;
To honourable *Dorset* now espows'd,   95
In whose faire breast true virtue then was hous'd:
Oh what delight did my weake spirits find
In those pure parts of her well framed mind:
And yet it grieves me that I cannot be
Neere unto her, whose virtues did agree   100
With those faire ornaments of outward beauty,
Which did enforce from all both love and dutie.
Unconstant Fortune, thou art most too blame,
Who casts us downe into so lowe a frame:
Where our great friends we cannot dayly see,   105
So great a diffrence is there in degree.
Many are placed in those Orbes of state,
Parters in honour, so ordain'd by Fate;
Neerer in show, yet farther off in love,
In which, the lowest alwayes are above.   110
But whither am I carried in conceit?

Lines 91–92. **Joseph … need**: son of Israel sold by his brothers into Egypt, he became powerful and his brothers petitioned him for food during the great famine (Gen. 37:42–45).

Lines 93–95. **Lady … espows'd**: Anne, Countess of Dorset, the Countess of Cumberland's daughter. She was the product of two great families: the Cliffords, earls of Cumberland (on her father's side) and the Russells, earls of Bedford (on her mother's); she had married into a third, the Sackvilles, earls of Dorset.

Line 103. **Fortune**: fate, circumstance.   Line 105. **great**: noble.

Line 106. **degree**: social status.   Line 107. **Orbes of state**: political world.

Line 108. **Parters in honour**: separated by rank.

Lines 109–10. **Neerer … above**: circumstance may place the high and low near to each other, but their devotion is not reciprocally strong; the lower born are more devoted to the high than the reverse.

My Wit too weake to conster of the great.
Why not? although we are but borne of earth,
We may behold the Heavens, despising death;
And loving heaven that is so farre above,   115
May in the end vouchsafe us entire love.
Therefore sweet Memorie doe thou retaine
Those pleasures past, which will not turne againe:
Remember beauteous *Dorsets* former sports,
So farre from beeing toucht by ill reports;   120
Wherein my selfe did alwaies beare a part,
While reverend Love presented my true heart:
Those recreations let me beare in mind,
Which her sweet youth and noble thoughts did finde:
Whereof depriv'd, I evermore must grieve,   125
Hating blind Fortune, carelesse to relieve.
And you sweet Cooke-ham, whom these Ladies leave,
I now must tell the griefe you did conceave
At their departure; when they went away,
How every thing retaind a sad dismay: 130
Nay long before, when once an inkeling came,
Me thought each thing did unto sorrow frame:
The trees that were so glorious in our view,
Forsooke both flowres and fruit, when once they knew
Of your depart, their very leaves did wither,   135
Changing their colours as they grewe together.
But when they saw this had no powre to stay you,

Line 112. **conster**: consider, understand.

Line 119. **Dorsets**: Anne's (see lines 93–95).

Line 120. **So ... reports**: Anne's activities were blameless, innocent fun, in which Lanyer shared (line 121).

Line 128. **conceave**: develop.   Line 131. **inkeling**: small idea.

They often wept, though speechlesse, could not
    pray you;
Letting their teares in your faire bosoms fall,
As if they said, Why will ye leave us all?   140
This being vaine, they cast their leaves away,
Hoping that pitie would have made you stay:
Their frozen tops like Ages hoarie haires,
Showes their disasters, languishing in feares:
A swarthy riveld ryne all over spread,   145
Their dying bodies halfe alive, halfe dead.
But your occasions call'd you so away,
That nothing there had power to make you stay:
Yet did I see a noble gratefull minde,
Requiting each according to their kind,   150
Forgetting not to turne and take your leave
Of these sad creatures, powrelesse to receive
Your favour when with griefe you did depart,
Placing their former pleasures in your heart;
Giving great charge to noble Memory,   155
There to preserve their love continually:
But specially the love of that faire tree,
That first and last you did vouchsafe to see:
In which it pleas'd you oft to take the ayre,
With noble *Dorset*, then a virgin faire: 160
Where many a learned Booke was read and skand
To this faire tree, taking me by the hand,
You did repeat the pleasures which had past,

Line 138. **pray you**: beg you (to stay).   Line 141. **vaine**: useless.

Line 143. **hoarie**: white.   Line 145. **swarthy ... ryne**: dark rough covering.

Line 147. **occasions**: responsibilities.   Line 150. **Requiting**: rewarding.

Line 160. **then ... faire**: before Anne's marriage.

Seeming to grieve they could no longer last.
And with a chaste, yet loving kisse tooke leave,   165
Of which sweet kisse I did it soone bereave:
Scorning a sencelesse creature should possesse
So rare a favour, so great happinesse.
No other kisse it could receive from me,
For feare to give backe what it tooke of thee: 170
So I ingratefull Creature did deceive it,
Of that which you vouchsaft in love to leave it.
And though it oft had giv'n me much content,
Yet this great wrong I never could repent:
But of the happiest made it most forlorne,   175
To shew that nothing's free from Fortunes scorne,
While all the rest with this most beauteous tree,
Made their sad consort Sorrowes harmony.
The floures that on the banks and walkes did grow,
Crept in the ground, the Grasse did weepe for woe.   180
The Windes and Waters seem'd to chide together,
Because you went away they know not whither:
And those sweet Brookes that ranne so faire and cleare,
With griefe and trouble wrinckled did appeare.
Those pretty Birds that wonted were to sing,   185
Now neither sing, nor chirp, nor use their wing;
But with their tender feet on some bare spray,
Warble forth sorrow, and their owne dismay.
Faire *Philomela* leaves her mournefull Ditty,

Line 166. **Of ... bereave**: Lanyer claims to have kissed the tree after the Countess, and so deprived the tree of the Countess's kiss.

Line 167. **sencelesse**: without feelings.   Line 171. **deceive**: deprive.

Line 172. **vouchsaft**: were willing.   Line 175. **forlorne**: sorrowful.

Line 178. **consort**: company, with pun on consort as musical group.

Line 185. **wonted**: accustomed.   Line 189. **Ditty**: song.

Drownd in dead sleepe, yet can procure no pittie: 190
Each arbour, banke, each seate, each stately tree,
Lookes bare and desolate now for want of thee;
Turning greene tresses into frostie gray,
While in cold griefe they wither all away.
The Sunne grew weake, his beames no comfort gave,   195
While all greene things did make the earth their grave:
Each brier, each bramble, when you went away,
Caught fast your clothes, thinking to make you stay:
Delightfull Eccho wonted to reply
To our last words, did now for sorrow die: 200
The house cast off each garment that might grace it,
Putting on Dust and Cobwebs to deface it.
All desolation then there did appeare,
When you were going whom they held so deare.
This last farewell to *Cooke-ham* here I give,   205
When I am dead thy name in this may live,
Wherein I have perform'd her noble hest,
Whose virtues lodge in my unworthy breast,
And ever shall, so long as life remaines,
Tying my heart to her by those rich chaines.   210

Line 192. **want**: lack.   Line 193. **tresses**: leaves.   Line 197. **brier**: briar bush.

Line 199. **Eccho**: wood nymph, personification of the effect.

Line 207. **her**: the Countess of Cumberland's.

Line 210. **those rich chaines**: of her virtues.

To the doubtfull Reader

Gentle Reader, if thou desire to be resolved, why I give this Title, *Salve Deus Rex Judæorum*, know for certaine; that it was delivered unto me in sleepe many yeares before I had any intent to write in this maner, and was quite out of my memory, untill I had written the Passion of Christ, when immediately it came into my remembrance, what I had dreamed long before; and thinking it a significant token, that I was appointed to performe this Worke, I gave the very same words I received in sleepe as the fittest Title I could devise for this Booke.

Title. **doubtfull**: doubting; curious.
Line 7. **token**: sign; message.   **performe**: produce; write.